MODERN PUEBLO POTTERY

NORTHLAND PRESS / FLAGSTAFF

MODERN PUEBLO POTTERY
1880-1960

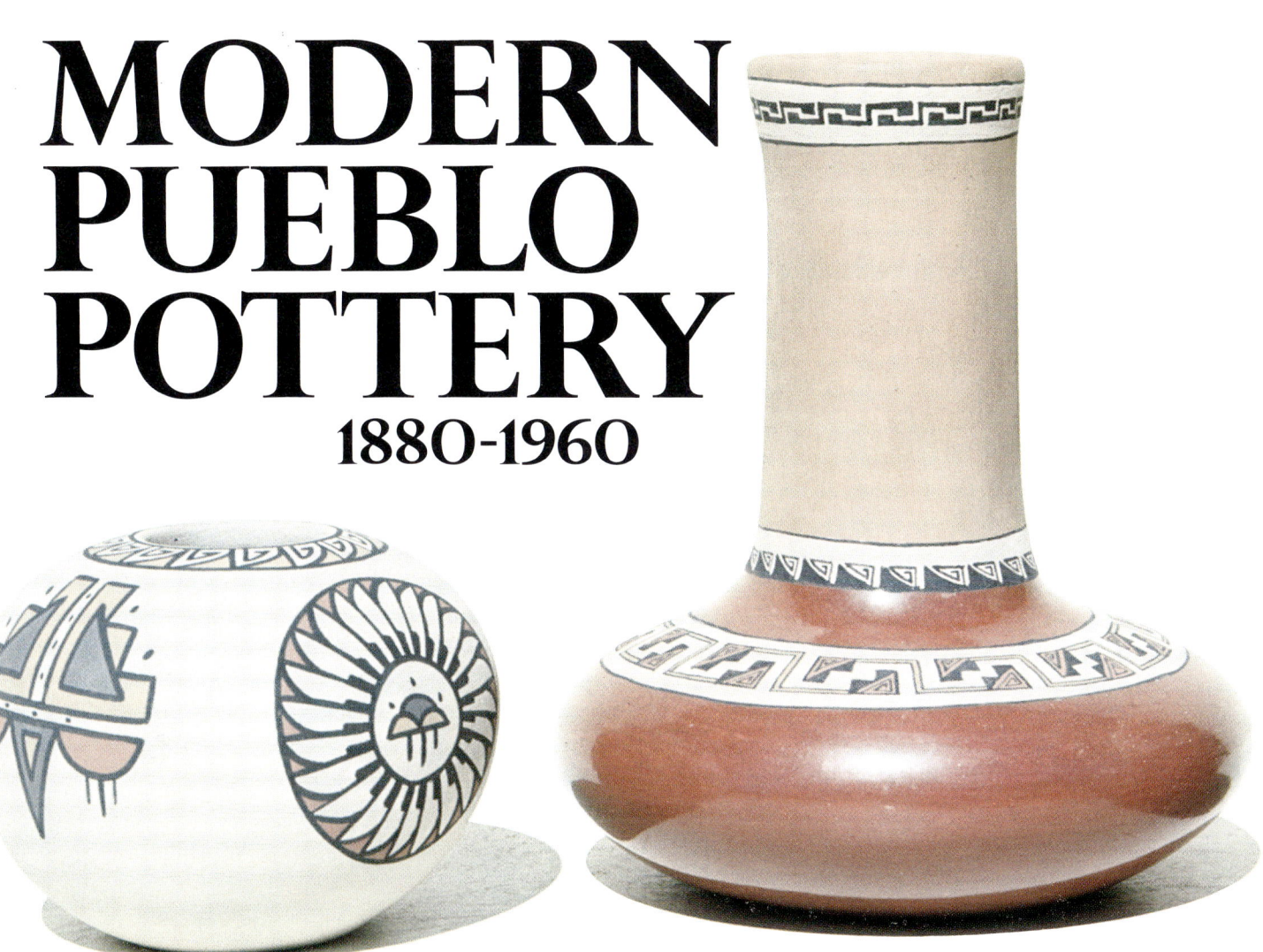

by Francis H. Harlow

Title page. SANTA CLARA: *Three modern polychrome vessels. Left, a white-slip bowl by Sunbird; middle, a jar by Lois — Derek; right, a low bowl by Petra. Circa 1975. Height, 10 cm., 21.5 cm., 8 cm.* — Bob Ward

Copyright © 1977 by Francis H. Harlow
All Rights Reserved

FIRST EDITION

ISBN 0-87358-159-8
Library of Congress Catalog Card Number 76-52540
Composed and Printed in the United States of America

CONTENTS

PREFACE vii	Santo Domingo 52
INTRODUCTION 1	Cochiti 56
The Pueblo Indians 1	THE PUNAME PUEBLOS 63
Indian Pottery 2	Jemez 63
Pottery Manufacture 2	Santa Ana 65
Types of Pottery 6	Zia 69
The Forms and Uses of Pueblo Pottery . 7	THE WESTERN KERES PUEBLOS . 75
CHRONOLOGY 11	Acoma 75
The Prehistoric Era (500 A.D.–1600 A.D.) 11	Laguna 81
The Historic Era (1600 A.D.–Present) . 13	THE ASHIWI PUEBLOS 85
THE NORTHERN TIWA PUEBLOS 21	THE HOPI PUEBLOS 91
Taos and Picuris 21	THE OTHER SOUTHWESTERN INDIANS 97
THE TEWA PUEBLOS 25	Maricopa 97
San Juan 25	Mojave 98
Santa Clara 27	Papago 99
San Ildefonso 34	Navajo 100
Nambe and Pojoaque 43	GLOSSARY 103
Tesuque 45	SELECTED READING 107
THE NORTHEAST KERES PUEBLOS 51	INDEX 109
San Felipe 51	

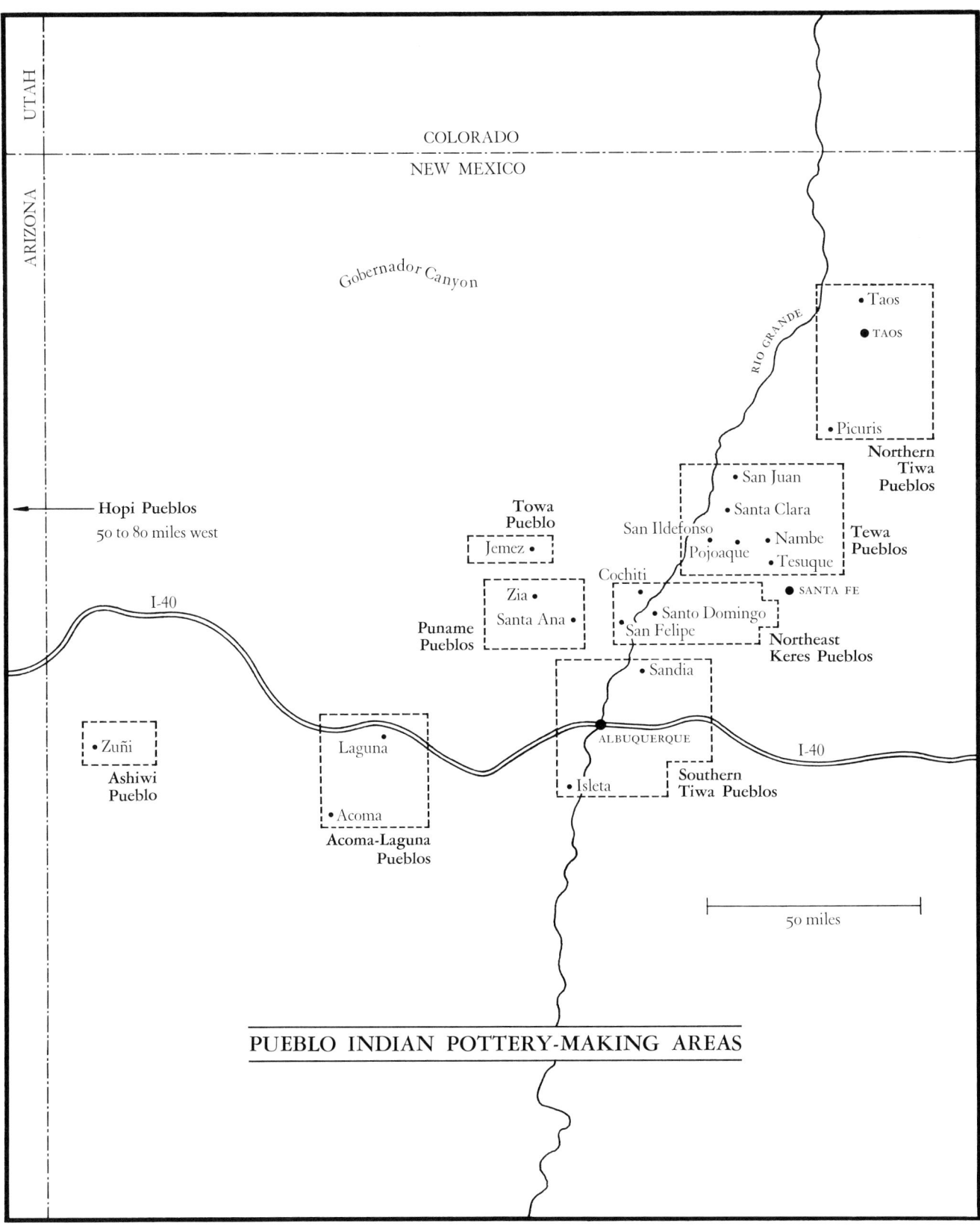

PREFACE

A PERSONAL VIEW

The aesthetic appeal of Pueblo Indian pottery lies in sensing its traditions, in observing its forms and designs, in smelling its earthy fragrance, in feeling the curves and textures of its surfaces, and most of all in associating the vessels with people, life and the mystic roots of nature. A brand-new pot may be dazzling in its virtuoso creation from the simplest materials of earth and vegetation. But let it age with dignity, acquire the chips and fractures of loving use, be rubbed by countless hands and permeated with the sweat and oils of honest human labor; let it assist in all the mysteries of prayer and supplication to the gods for rain, for appeasement and thanksgiving, for celebrations of joy and beauty, for relief from suffering; let its familiar appearance burn into the hearts and memories of half a dozen generations; then the vessel and the people and the village and all the surrounding fields and rivers and mountains become one being, and if you can sense all this you are close to understanding the real essence of Pueblo Indian pottery.

The people of the pueblos sense it. I've seen them visit a fine collection and recognize a venerable pot of their village traditions. I've watched their gentle greeting of the vessel as they fill themselves with its presence. I've seen the way old pots were mended by the native people, using all the skill at their command, just as earnestly as the healing man would treat a patient, in both cases seeking to preserve a precious, irreplaceable life.

I'm not an Indian, except in the tiniest fraction of my blood. My vocation in the fields of mathematics and physics brings me into daily contact with the realities of modern life, and with the practical goals of professional and financial achievement. Perhaps I would have met with greater success in those pursuits if not for the more irrational traits that make me a dreamer, and have led me to studies of pottery and art. But for me, the examination of a fine pot or the creation of a beautiful painting is as exciting as the development of a valid new mathematical theory, and the aesthetic sensations of life, talent, personality and humanity are even more awesome and important.

My studies of pottery are infused with a sense of scientific order, as the text of this book clearly shows. Indeed, for me the world of words is much better handled when the purposes are purely objective and technical. The notebooks in my mind abound with observations and feelings related to the people and places I've seen along the way: Indians, traders, collectors, anthropologists, dealers, tourists, modern villages, ancient ruins, museums, dusty corners here and there, sunshine, turquoise skies, snow on the piñon trees, the fragrance of juniper smoke, quiet afternoons in a

PREFACE

pueblo, Indian friends, and just plain silence. I've tried to write these down but the words play tricks and distort the intentions. I'll tell you about them in person some day, if you come to visit and are patient enough to listen. But even if we never meet, I hope that you can take a moment where you are to look and feel and smell an Indian pot, and listen deep inside yourself to all it has to say.

ACKNOWLEDGMENTS

The manuscript has profited from the critical readings and suggestions by Forrest Fenn, John Rivenburgh, and especially my wife, Patricia Harlow. I am also grateful to countless Indian friends, archaeologists, museum curators, collectors, traders and shop proprietors for sharing their knowledge, experience and storehouse of lore, and especially to Maria Martinez and her talented family who have opened their home to me on numerous occasions and given me access to their extensive knowledge of the evolution of San Ildefonso ceramics developments.

In Santa Fe, The Museum of New Mexico, George Ewing, Director, and the School of American Research, Douglas Schwartz, Director, have granted me continuing access to their superb pottery collections and permitted me to photograph vessels for this book. Arthur Olivas has been of great help with The Museum's extensive library of old photographs. Betty Toulouse and Nancy Fox have been very helpful and patient during my work with the collections for this study.

In addition, I wish to thank the following organizations and people for permission to study and photograph Indian pottery in their collections:

Fenn Galleries, Ltd., Forrest Fenn, Director;
Santa Fe Village Art Museum,
   Nicholas Woloshuk, Director;
Bob Ward Indian Traders,
   Bob Ward, Director;
Ford Ruthling;
John Rivenburgh;
Packard's Chaparral Trading Post,
   Al Packard, Director;
Spencer MacCallum;
An anonymous collector, to whom I owe a
   special note of thanks.

Finally, I wish to express my particular appreciation to the Fenn Galleries, Ltd., for their generous auspices in sponsoring the writing of this book. Many essential tasks have been performed on behalf of the publication by Forrest Fenn and John Rivenburgh.

FRANCIS H. HARLOW
Los Alamos, New Mexico

INTRODUCTION

The Pueblo Indians

The modern Pueblo Indians of Arizona and New Mexico are the descendants of a long line of people who have been living nearby for at least two thousand years. Some of their present villages have been occupied continuously for eight centuries while older habitations lie in ruins all about.

Archaeologists are beginning to piece together the ancient history of these early Americans, prior to the time that they began to settle in permanent houses. Until then, they were hunters and gatherers, traveling from place to place in search of food and shelter, fashioning little more than they could carry with them, and expending most of their available time and energy on mere subsistence.

Then, shortly before the time of Christ, a change occurred. As happened many other times around the world, the pace of civilization began to quicken. A new way of life emerged. Instead of constantly searching for nature's capricious gifts of food, the people learned to plant their crops. No longer forced to move about, they could build permanent houses, stay in one place for years, enjoy a bit of leisure, and accumulate some material possessions.

Today the Southwestern United States is covered with many thousands of ancient ruined houses and tiny villages. The earlier ones are seldom larger than a few rooms in size. The later ones, dating after the tenth century, are often much larger, with five hundred rooms or more.

Constructed of stone, logs, and mud, these flat-topped buildings can be very comfortable, cool in the hot summer and warm in the winter. The setting may be on the top of a wild and scarcely accessible mesa, or in the protection of a large overhanging cliff. Sometimes extra rooms were carved into the soft rock itself. The Spanish explorers called the little towns pueblos, from which we derive the most common name for these people, the Pueblo Indians.

The name implies, however, more homogeneity than is really justified. In the ancient ruins we see numerous regional variations in architecture, and in the remains of material possessions. The languages spoken by the modern descendants show strong variations, some as distinct from each other as English and Chinese.

Today, instead of thousands of pueblos there are only nineteen in New Mexico and half that many in northeastern Arizona. Many factors contributed to the decline, a drought in the thirteenth century, consolidation of small settlements into a few larger ones, raiding by Apaches, Navajos and other Indians commencing in the sixteenth century, and strife with Europeans in the seventeenth and eighteenth centuries. Seemingly headed for oblivion by the middle of the nineteenth century, the Pueblo Indians instead began to thrive, and through the past hundred years the populations of their villages have been increasing rapidly.

Today, the Pueblo Indians retain more of their traditional ways of life than any other of the United States tribes, excepting perhaps some of the Eskimos. Many European traits are being assimilated, however, and perhaps the uniquely Indian ways will eventually be lost, but for the present a visit to an Indian pueblo is a trip into history.

Indian Pottery

The subject of this book is modern pottery of the Pueblo Indians, and of the neighboring Indian tribes in the southwestern states of Arizona and New Mexico. By modern pottery we mean from the period 1880 to the present. The preceding styles are also discussed briefly in this book, and more thoroughly in two other recent books.* Here, we emphasize both the artistry and the traditions of this venerable craft, and discuss just enough of the technical details to satisfy most serious collectors.

The roots of modern Pueblo Indian pottery are like those of ancient civilizations throughout the world. Whenever "Stone-Age" people begin to settle into villages anywhere in the world, they also start to enjoy a new degree of leisure and to experience the fruits that come from division of labor. Handicrafts flourish, among them stone carving, weaving, and pottery making. In the Near East, this period was nearly ten thousand years ago, in Asia about five thousand years ago, in Central America and Peru it was a few hundred years before the time of Christ, and in the Pueblo Indian world the beginning of this period was about two thousand years in the past.

Matte-Paint Pottery by F. H. Harlow, Museum of New Mexico Press, Santa Fe, 1973; *Historic Pottery of the Pueblo Indians 1600–1880* by L. Frank and F. H. Harlow, New York Graphic Society, Boston, 1974.

Everywhere at this stage of civilization, pottery making is accomplished with only the simplest materials and tools. Yet at its finest, these wares can be both extremely beautiful and completely serviceable. The Pueblo Indians have the distinction of making pottery that was rarely surpassed in excellence by any of the comparable Old World cultures.

Pottery Manufacture

The techniques used by the pueblo potters for making their wares have changed very little since prehistoric days. Even the vessels being produced by many of the modern potters are made by traditional materials and methods, although some recent innovations have utilized both commercial materials and tools.

Clay is plentiful throughout the area. In most places, the clay is too pure and must be mixed with an inert material (the temper) to keep the clay from being excessively sticky or cracking as it dries.

The traditions regarding what to use for the tempering material are very important to each village. At Zia Pueblo, for example, finely crushed black basalt has been used invariably for centuries, imparting a black peppery appearance to the brick-red fired clay. The result is a unique means of identification for pottery from that village. In contrast, at Acoma and Zuñi Pueblos pieces of old, broken pottery are crushed to fine powder and mixed with the clay to give a distinctive, finely chunky texture. With a little practice, one can learn to recognize these variations in appearance, which are discussed in more detail in the chapters on each ceramics area.

After the clay has been cleaned, mixed with temper and water, and allowed to "cure" for a while, it is ready to be modeled into the form of a jar, bowl, or other shape. For this purpose, no potter's wheel is used, although a mold for the base of the vessel is often employed, and this may

Hopi: *A view of Walpi Pueblo, photographed by Ben Wittick, circa 1890.* — Museum of New Mexico Photo Archives

be rotated by hand as the wall of the vessel is built. To the clay forming the base are added ropes of clay, coiled around to build up the wall.

After the material has dried somewhat, the wall is thinned to the desired extent by scraping or, in the southwestern desert tribes, by slapping with a wooden paddle while a rock or other smooth object is held inside as an anvil. The surface is then well smoothed.

The usual next step for decorated pottery is to apply red or white slip to the exterior surface, and to the interior if the vessel has a wide mouth. The slip is a watery suspension of very fine clay, which accomplishes several purposes. First, it hides the coarser, less attractive body material. Second, it can be polished to form a less porous (but not impermeable) surface to impede leakage after firing. Third, it serves to receive the pigments used for decorating the pot, absorbing or binding them more securely than the basic clay. On some decorated pottery types, for example many of the Hopi Indian styles, no slip is used or necessary, as the basic clay itself can be nicely polished and painted. In no traditional style is the surface ever completely glazed; even the shiniest of the polished black pottery is finished with a slip. Rarely one encounters modern glazed pots in Pueblo Indian style, but these and other departures from tradition are not discussed in this book. Prior to 1700, some Indian pottery was decorated with a mineral paint that melted during the firing and resolidified to a shiny, vitreous surface qualifying as a true glaze. Such pottery was not treated this way for overall waterproofing, but rather because the effect was visually pleasing in the design lines for which it was used. The technique was only recently rediscovered by a non-Indian craftsman, after being "lost" for nearly three centuries.

INTRODUCTION

The slipped surface, or the basic clay if unslipped, is polished in either of two ways. One is with a smooth stone, patiently rubbed over the damp slip until it is well compacted and glossy. Sometimes if the pot is not to have painted designs, animal fat is used in the final phase of stone polishing. The polishing stones are treasured heirlooms, passed through many generations, until their surfaces are worn flat.

The other way to polish is with a piece of hide or fabric. Some potters are very skillful with rag polishing, but sometimes the result is striate and not as attractive as stone polishing.

Two types of paint are traditionally used for the decoration of Pueblo Indian pottery, vegetal and mineral. Vegetal paint is made by boiling succulent spring leaves and stems, especially of the Rocky Mountain bee plant. The thick brownish juice is dried into cakes of a material called guaco, and then dissolved with water when needed. Mineral paints are of various types. For black or dark brown, an iron mineral is commonly used. Red, orange, tan and similar earth colors are achieved by means of various clays. The red color is usually the same as the clay which is used for an overall red slip.

Vegetal paint soaks into the polished slip and chars to a black color when fired. Sugar water or almost any similar carbonaceous compound would also serve the purpose. Since the material soaks in, the surface retains its polish.

The mineral paints, in contrast, adhere to the surface. Except for the ancient glazing minerals, the result for the black design lines is a dull, or matte, finish. Mineral paints usually show tinges of brownish color, whereas the vegetal paints are sooty black.

As with the tempering material, the type of paint at any one village is a persistent tradition, which also assists in identifying the pueblo of origin for a pot.

In recent years, however, some pueblo potters have departed from the traditional paint of their village, even to the extent of using commercial poster paints, applied after the vessel has been fired. The number of variations is rapidly increasing, and will be mentioned briefly in the discussions of the various pottery-making areas and villages.

The final step in making a pot is the firing. The traditional technique is to fire the vessels outdoors on the ground when the weather is calm and clear. Typically the ground is warmed by a preliminary fire, and a supporting structure is built of stones or sheets of metal and wire. The pots are placed there upside down, and the fuel is piled over. Fuel usually consists of dried dung, slabs of bark, kindling, wood, and sometimes other materials.

Two basically different firing sequences are used, referred to as reducing and oxidizing. In both cases the fire usually has a reducing (or smudging) atmosphere in the early stages. This means that oxygen is effectively excluded from the central part of the fire where the pottery is located, so that the chemistry of the various minerals results in compounds that are poor in oxygen. If this condition persists through the entire firing process, that is, if the fire is never allowed to burn all the fuel with a good draft of air but instead is kept closed and smoldering, then any red slip or paint turns dark gray or black, and white slips or clay become cool shades of light gray. This type of reducing fire was especially prevalent during the earlier prehistoric days, until the thirteenth century, and is used in modern times to achieve the polished black wares that have brought fame to the northern Rio Grande pueblos.

An oxidizing fire allows for a draft of oxygen-rich air to bathe the vessels during the late stages of firing, converting many chemical compounds to oxides. As a result, red slip and paint become a warm brick-red color, and white slips are tinged with shades of cream, tan, orange, yellow and similar earth colors. The only remaining black is from the vegetal paint, or from certain mineral

SANTA CLARA: *A sacred dance, photographed by William Regan, circa 1963.* — Los Alamos Scientific Laboratory

paints, which actually are very dark brown rather than jet black.

If the oxygen-rich flame occurs only briefly at the end of the firing, then the core of the clay may still retain the dark gray appearance of the reducing phase. If a piece of fuel lying against the pot during the oxidizing phase is not completely burned, then the surface at that point may remain reduced, resulting in a "fire cloud." Such smudged-looking areas were not considered by the Indians to be serious blemishes until the purpose of pottery making began to emphasize beauty for commercial sales purposes. Neither the fire clouds nor the overall black is soot, which could rub off like carbon from a candle flame. The dark color is the result of chemical changes in the clay and its associated impurities, and is therefore quite permanent.

In recent years, the Pueblo Indians have found through experimentation that the richest black

SAN ILDEFONSO: *Santana Martinez polishes the slip with a smooth stone. Photograph, 1964, by William Regan.* — Los Alamos Scientific Laboratory

SAN ILDEFONSO: *Santana Martinez shows how designs are painted onto the polished slip. Photograph, 1964, by William Regan.* — Los Alamos Scientific Laboratory

colors from a reduced firing can be achieved if the maximum temperature is kept low, less than 700°C. For optimal hardening of the clay, however, the more traditional temperature of greater than 850° is required. With commercial sales a primary goal, the result has been to emphasize beauty over strength, so that much of the modern black pottery is cool-fired and accordingly not serviceable, and will even tend to decompose if wetted. A similar dilemma occurs with oxidized firings. In that case, experience shows that uniformity of color and the avoidance of fire clouds can be controlled better with a cooler fire, so that in this case, too, we find that the modern pueblo colored pottery produced for display, artistry and sale may also be relatively soft and unserviceable.

The contrast with earlier wares in regard to strength and household service is marked. Pueblo pottery made prior to about 1880 is almost always strong and stands up well to hard wear. After about 1880 some villages and some individual potters in other villages continued to emphasize these traditional attributes. Again this is a matter that will be discussed in more detail in the chapters on the various pottery areas and villages.

Types of Pottery

Stylistic developments in the history of Pueblo Indian pottery are usually described in terms of a sequence of pottery "types." The idea of associating all similar vessels with a type name is very useful. The name itself always has two parts, the first derived from a geographical location and the second usually describing a general attribute of appearances. Examples are:

  Flagstaff Black-on-white
  Zuñi Polychrome

The designation of a type name is accomplished by formal publication of the attributes that define the type, including the time period and place of its manufacture, the variations that can be expected, and any other information that helps to establish the uniqueness and validity of the name designated.

The reason type names are useful is the remarkable fact that no southwestern pottery type has ever been exactly duplicated outside of the area and time period of its principal manufacture. To give perspective to the situation, a typical pottery type might have been made for about fifty years and in an area fifty miles across. Of course there are numerous variations, some types having been made only briefly and others for as long as several hundred years. Some were made only in one small village and others across a hundred miles or more.

Usually there were several types of pottery being made simultaneously in each area. We don't know if each potter made all of the types or if they were made by different individuals, or perhaps even by different villages. In any case, within the time and region for a particular type, there is a remarkable uniformity in its features, attributable to a rigidly conservative outlook that has characterized the Southwestern Indians until the most recent decades.

The two features, consistent uniformity and lack of duplication, are what give meaning and value to the concept of Indian pottery types. Only in recent years, with much experimentation by the Indian craftsman on a large variety of new styles, has the concept of pottery type become somewhat clouded. Thus, while we can easily discuss virtually every ceramic piece made before about 1960 in terms of a relatively simple system of classification, our descriptions of the recent innovations have to be less systematic.

The Forms and Uses of Pueblo Pottery

Each type of Indian pottery has usually been made in several different forms, each with its specific purpose. Bowls and jars for cooking and serving food are among the most common forms encountered from the period prior to about 1900. At all times, however, there have been many variations developed for specific purposes other than everyday domestic use.

To some extent, the quality of a vessel is also associated with the purpose for which it was intended. Cooking vessels, for example, were usually not decorated or even carefully smoothed on the outside, since the fire would mar the appearance during usage, but the interior was often well-smoothed or even polished to facilitate cleaning.

In general, the quality is high in those attributes that are currently of importance, and suffer in the rest. In the current century the emphasis is on beautiful appearance, with strength and lightness having little value. In earlier periods we find similar examples of this effect. During easy and pleasant circumstances, for example, the pottery may be quite sloppy in appearance, whereas adversity would be accompanied by the production of very beautiful wares. In such cases, the artistry or lack of it could have been associated with the need for favor with the gods. Drought, disease or war would require strengthening the power of all chants, prayers, dances and other ceremonial acts. The associated paraphernalia would have to be reworked and new finer costumes and vessels fashioned from the available materials. But during good times the need for appeasing the gods would decrease and sloppiness set in again.

We have no way of knowing for sure if this explanation is correct, but the circumstantial evidence is strong. During the drought in northeastern Arizona in the last quarter of the thirteenth century, for example, the Kayenta branch of the Pueblo Indians developed superb new pottery types, such as Kayenta Polychrome, and established the roots for the fine pottery that characterized Hopi wares for several centuries thereafter. Likewise, following the massacre of Acoma Indians by the Spanish at the beginning of the seventeenth century, there arose one of the finest glaze-ware types ever made by "Stone-Age" people anywhere in the world. Even more widespread are the superb ceramics made throughout the Pueblo area during the classical period following the Pueblo Revolt of 1680 and the subsequent reconquest by De Vargas and his soldiers. In this last case, the abundant occurrence of sacred feather symbols during this period is especially significant.

To illustrate the association of form with usage, the following list includes a variety of the more common examples.

1. HOUSEHOLD BOWL. This simple, rounded, wide-mouth form has been used for many centuries. Numerous minor variations serve to distinguish the current style, but the idea is always the same. Small bowls, up to ten centimeters in diameter, are relatively uncommon, their purpose usually having been for special ceremonial occasions. Middle-size bowls, from ten to forty centimeters in diameter, are among the most common of the decorated pueblo pottery forms prior to about 1880. From 600 A.D. countless numbers were produced for domestic service until factory wares began to replace the native dishes in the nineteenth century. Large bowls, with diameter exceeding forty centimeters, are again less common. Usually called dough bowls, they were seldom made before about 1760. Surviving examples often have bits of bread dough stuck on the interior, purposefully left to pass their spirit onto the next batch.

2. HOUSEHOLD JAR. With relatively tall proportions and narrow neck, the jar is also an ancient and widely manufactured form. The variation that has a handle on one side, called a pitcher, has also been made for household use, especially during the prehistoric era. Again, the most common size has medium measurements, from twenty to thirty centimeters in height. Smaller jars were more rare until this century, when they have been produced in abundance for commercial sales. The traditional medium-size jars are usually called water jars. Since about 1700 such vessels almost always have a concave base for carrying on the head, a feature that arose in the prehistoric villages near modern Santa Fe during the fifteenth century and gradually spread to all but the Hopi Pueblos. Very large jars, typically fifty centimeters or more in height, are called storage jars. They, too, were seldom made before about 1760, although some truly remarkable prehistoric examples are known. These venerable ceramic giants were seldom moved from the shelter of back storage rooms, where dried edibles were stored in them during harvest and removed as needed through the winter. Because of their protection, many fine examples survive from the nineteenth century, sometimes strengthened by rawhide tied around to prevent cracking, and sometimes speckled with candle-wax drippings accidentally spilled during the dark days of winter.

3. CEREMONIAL VESSELS. Usually departing in freedom and design from the household pots, the sacred vessels have been especially distinctive in appearance during the historic era. In ancient days, perhaps every decorated pot was sacred, but the Catholic zeal to prevent idolatry apparently induced a more clear-cut distinction between the secular vessels used for everyday household purposes and the sacred vessels that were carefully hidden from the European settlers. Some prehistoric pots were clearly special in their ceremonial function. These are frequently in the form of tiny jars, or, rarely, effigies in human or animal form. The ancient "duck" pots, however, are thought to have simply been urinals for use at night, although there seems to be no conclusive proof of this speculation. Before the Europeans forbade the custom, pottery was often buried with the dead. The vessels were usually the household utensils, which otherwise apparently had no special significance. In the ruins at Casas Grandes, however, many of the pots found in graves are elaborate effigy vessels, with strange human and animal forms, which look as though they were made specifically for burial because they show no signs of household wear. The twelfth-century Mimbres

Three Pueblo Indian vessels showing unusual forms. Left, dipper of Homolovi Polychrome, circa 1325; center, Zuñi prayer-meal bowl, circa 1910; right, Tesuque ceremonial bowl, circa 1890. — Painting by Francis Harlow

INTRODUCTION

Indians often "killed" their burial bowls by punching a hole through the bottom, but this habit was neither long-lasting nor widespread. Ceremonial vessels from the historic era often have unusual forms, for example rectangular, or sculpture such as a stair-step on the rim. Many such vessels survive from the pueblo of Zuñi, but examples from other villages such as Zia and Laguna are exceedingly rare. Because of the traditional limitation of many ceremonial activities to men, it is thought that many of the ceremonial vessels were decorated by men, although the actual manufacture of pottery is typically women's work.

4. COMMERCIAL POTS. The Pueblo Indians have made pottery for sale or barter for at least fourteen centuries. Even during the prehistoric era, the emphasis in vessels made for widespread export from a village was on beauty, and it was almost always the most artistic of the wares that saw the furthest dissemination. The ceramics skills of the ancient Hopis, for example, resulted in the trading of their vessels to all parts of the Pueblo world and beyond, and at the same time stimulated excellence seldom equalled by their contemporaries. During the historic era, the same effect can be detected at Zia Pueblo, which traded pottery for much of its food from the nearby villages of Jemez, Santa Ana, and San Felipe. In the modern periods, and especially in the last decade, the commercial aspects of pueblo pottery manufacture have become predominant, and again the emphasis has been on beauty. The best results are exquisite, revealing an apex of Pueblo Indian artistry in both form and decoration, almost invariably, however, at the complete sacrifice of those attributes that would previously have been required to make them useful. Nevertheless, it is exactly this response, this Indian adaptability to the circumstances at hand, that demonstrate how traditional in its own way the modern ceramic trends really are. Modern tourists* and collectors are scarcely different from the ancient traders. The only change in circumstances is that during this last century there has been, for the first time, almost no demand for pottery for domestic use.

---

*See Glossary for the context of this word in this book.

CHRONOLOGY

The Prehistoric Era
(500 A.D.-1600 A.D.)

The earliest decorated pottery produced by the ancestors of the Pueblo Indians was made around 500 A.D. For some hundreds of years, the desert tribes in the southern part of what is now Arizona and New Mexico had been making pottery in colors of brown or buff, and decorating it with a mineral paint that fired to various shades of brick red. We do not know how much the ancestral Pueblo Indians learned from their southern neighbors about this new craft, but the influence must have been appreciable. Nevertheless there was also some northern innovation. Instead of red-on-buff or red-on-brown pots, most of the Basketmakers, as the ancestral Puebloans are called, used a reducing fire to produce light gray vessels with black decorations.

Through the next several centuries, the Basketmakers evolved into the earliest of the true Pueblo Indians, but the black-on-gray and black-on-white traditions persisted with few exceptions until about 1000 A.D.

One exception occurred in the area of southwestern Colorado, where the potters produced red-on-orange pottery, which may have been influenced by the styles from the south and indeed may even indicate the migration of a group of southerners to these remote northern settlements.

By about 1000 A.D., a new idea for pottery decoration was discovered or else imported into the pueblo area from elsewhere. The technique required the entire vessel to be covered with a special slip that would fire to a red color. On this were painted black decorations, and the pot was fired in an oxidizing atmosphere. It appears that this new style was very pleasing to the Indians. Soon a number of variations appeared, for example, the partial omission of red slip, allowing the color of the body clay to show through. Another variant was to paint designs with white clay over the red, either by itself or as an edging to the black-line decorations.

These multi-color, or polychrome, styles spread rapidly, both through the trading about of individual vessels, and the copying of popular ideas. Many new pottery types evolved, distinguished from each other by the materials available in each region, by the various regional ideas in design layout and by changes in form, usually as a result of occasional spurts in the inventiveness of imaginative potters.

By about 1200 A.D., the colored wares achieved equal popularity to the more traditional black-on-white wares. By a century later the colored wares became overwhelmingly predominant, with the manufacture of black-on-white pottery being confined to few conservative areas, mainly along the Rio Grande, where it continued until as late as 1700.

During the ascendancy of the colored wares, the use of glaze paint was discovered. Even as early as 600 A.D., some of the black-firing mineral paints turned more or less vitreous during the firing, but the potentiality for beauty of designs was not consistently exploited until about 1250 A.D. The glazing material was never applied to the whole surface, but was confined, instead, to the dark-colored design lines, often in conjunction with red slip over the whole pot or as an accent or filling to the glaze lines. White-line designs or accents to design were also frequently employed, especially in the fourteenth century, when some exceptionally fine and beautiful pots were made.

The use of glaze paint continued until about 1700. The appearance became sloppy in some areas, especially the northern Rio Grande, but remained superb in others, especially at Acoma where the seventeenth century glaze-ware pots are among the finest ceramics ever made by the Pueblo Indians.

Through the glaze-paint period, many villages continued the traditional matte-paint styles, utilizing vegetal paint, or else minerals that did not vitrify during the firing. Outstanding among these mineral matte-paint styles is the Hopi Indian pottery type called Sikyatki Polychrome. With black and red designs on a polished bright yellow or yellow-orange background, the vessels of this type evoked admiration from both the Indians during the period of manufacture and the archaeologists who dug up these treasures many years later. Indeed, the inspiration given by these excavated vessels to the more recent Hopi Indians sparked a revival in excellence of pottery making during the late 1800s that has persisted to the present day.

All through the prehistoric era there also were manufactured a number of different utilitarian

Two ancient jars with black glaze paint. Left, Ramos Polychrome from Casa Grandes; right, Showlow Polychrome from east-central Arizona. Circa 1350. Height, 18.5 cm. and 10.5 cm.

styles of pottery. At some villages, the remains of these relatively plain and coarse vessels constitute as many as ninety-five percent of the pottery fragments uncovered by excavations. At others they are a small percentage. Rarely can they be considered artistic, although one class of utility wares, made principally in the period 1000 A.D.–1300 A.D. has examples that are truly works of exceptional skill and beauty. These are the corrugated vessels, made by coiling fine ropes of clay to build up the wall, and pinching each coil on the exterior of the pot to make a distinctive layered dimpling. The technique is very difficult, as proved by modern potters who have attempted to duplicate the ancient style but given up in frustration. The problem is that uniformity of coil size is very difficult to maintain, and it is hard to keep from bumping or smearing the partially completed surface while still soft. The modern copies that I have seen of this corrugated style are usually made by carving dimples into a pot that was formed and smoothed, so that the appearance only approximates the ancient corrugated look. In some areas, notably the Upper Gila River, a variant of this style during the twelfth century omitted most or all of the pinching, so that the vessels are circularly banded but not dimpled. The finest of these have almost incredibly fine bands, from the use of as many as sixteen ribbons of clay per inch. Sometimes these fine bands are also partially pinched to form complex designs.

The Historic Era
(1600 A.D.-PRESENT)

Several groups of Spanish explorers passed through the Southwestern Indian area during the sixteenth century, but the visits were brief and the effects, while surely vivid and exciting to the Indians, were nevertheless negligible in their influence on the local ceramics.

Not until 1598 was there a permanent European colony, settled by Juan de Oñate and a small

ZUNI: *A glaze-polychrome jar from the area of Hawikuh. Circa 1600. Height, 22.5 cm.* — Museum of New Mexico 3037/12

group of stalwart men and women at the confluence of the Rio Grande and Rio Chama, in the north-central part of what is now New Mexico. Twelve years later, the town of Santa Fe was established as the territorial capital, and it has remained the seat of government for the area through all the subsequent years of turmoil, which we call the Historic Era.

The fascinating history of Indian-European relations has been amply recorded elsewhere. Here we present a summary of the historic pottery-making periods, with brief mention of a few events that profoundly influenced the evolution of ceramic styles.

1. THE EARLY HISTORIC PERIOD, 1600–1700. Close continuity with prehistoric ceramic styles was the rule during the first century of European occupation. Glaze-ware pottery continued to be made in the middle Rio Grande pueblos and at Acoma and in the area of modern Zuñi. Also, Jemez Pueblo continued the anachronistic production of its ancient black-on-white pottery. Al-

LAGUNA: *Early Acomita Polychrome, showing the typical undercut underbody. Circa 1770. Height, 30.5 cm.*

JEMEZ BLACK-ON-WHITE: *A large jar with opposed handles. Circa 1600. Height, 35 cm.* — Museum of New Mexico 21913/11

together, the influence of the Europeans on the pueblo pottery styles was slight.

In 1680, the Indians revolted against the Spanish and succeeded in driving them from the area for twelve years. Following the reconquest, some of the pueblos were relocated and some new ones established. Profound changes occurred in the pueblo pottery styles, not because of Spanish influence, but perhaps to some extent as a symbol of defiance towards the Spanish.

2. THE CLASSIC PERIOD, 1700–1760. Glaze-paint pottery was no longer made, and some villages, like Jemez and San Felipe, ceased the manufacture of decorated pottery altogether. At others, however, the new styles that emerged at around 1700 are among the finest ever made by the Pueblo Indians. The jars and bowls of this period are distinguished by their sculptural subtleties. These are not sculptures in the sense of effigy figures. They consist of flaring rims, angular bends in the surface, concave bases, lips at the rim top, and various other features, never very prominent but always present on one or another of the types. Designs were executed with greater care than before. Sacred feather symbols were very commonly employed in the patterns, and red was used more exuberantly in the decorations. The outstanding pottery types are:

    Tewa area: Ogapoge Polychrome
                 Pojoaque Polychrome
                 Kapo Black
    Puname area: Puname Polychrome
    Acoma: Ako Polychrome
    Zuñi: Ashiwi Polychrome
    Hopi area: Payupki Polychrome

3. THE UTILITARIAN PERIOD, 1760–1820. Rather abruptly at about 1760, the styles of decorated pueblo pottery changed considerably, losing many of the earlier subtle features of sculpture and design precision, and becoming much more

utilitarian. The usual form for a jar became much more nearly spherical, with a small neck, while bowls became quite uniformly rounded, with a little outflare at the rim. The delicate feather symbols in the designs were replaced by heavier patterns, usually more abstract and geometrical in appearance. In isolated instances, one can find continuation of design precision and artistic sculpture to the vessel surfaces, as for example in the early vessels of Kiapkwa Polychrome at Zuñi and the jars of Santa Clara Black in the Tewa area. The major decorated pottery types of this period are:

    Tewa area: Powhoge Polychrome
    Northeast Keres area: Kiua Polychrome
    Puname area: San Pablo Polychrome
                    Ranchitos Polychrome
    Acoma-Laguna area: Acomita Polychrome
    Zuñi: Kiapkwa Polychrome

4. DECLINE AND TRANSITION PERIOD, 1820–1880. This period opens with the independence of Mexico from Spain and the establishment of trade routes with the United States. A host of new goods entered the area along the Santa Fe Trail, including dishes and pans. The demand for Indian pottery by the non-Indian inhabitants decreased sharply, and even the Indians themselves started to use a few of the imported wares. As a result and perhaps for other reasons, pueblos close to Santa Fe, like Nambe and San Ildefonso, almost ceased the manufacture of decorated wares. Even where the pueblo ceramics industry continued to flourish, there were various changes, and for them the period is more of transition than decline. Indeed, in some instances the craft experienced a distinct revival in both quality and artistry in the later parts of the period. A new freedom in design was initiated through the incorporation of birds, animals and floral patterns in the motifs. The outstanding pottery types are:

    Tewa area: Tesuque Polychrome
    Northeast Keres area: Cochiti Polychrome
                    Kiua Polychrome
    Puname area: Zia Polychrome
    Acoma-Laguna area: McCartys Polychrome
                    Laguna Polychrome
    Zuñi area: Zuñi Polychrome
    Hopi area: Polacca Polychrome
                Walpi Polychrome

5. THE COMMERCIAL REVIVAL PERIOD, 1880–1900. The new railroad of 1879 brought a flood of tourists, collectors, and anthropologists from the East, and the Pueblo Indians responded with the development of new styles emphasizing beauty rather than serviceability. San Ildefonso Polychrome was the principal new Tewa contribution, while in the Hopi area a woman named Nampeyo initiated a beautiful and famous pottery type called Hano Polychrome. It is this and the following periods that receive principal emphasis in this present book.

6. THE COMMERCIAL DECLINE PERIOD, 1900–1920. Disillusioned with the relatively poor quality that was an inevitable result of the tourist-

ACOMA: *A magnificent jar of Hawikuh Polychrome. Circa 1650. Height, 26 cm.* — Museum of New Mexico 3774/11

oriented flood of Indian ceramics, dealers and collectors decreased their purchases, and pueblo pottery making went into a period of considerable decline. Pueblos like Laguna and Zuñi have never recovered, their output becoming progressively less until only the smallest numbers of vessels have been produced after about 1920. In other villages the decline was temporary, with no irreparable damage.

7. THE RECENT PERIOD, 1920–1965. In the 1920s there was considerable interest among artists and anthropologists in the arts and crafts of the Pueblo Indians. An annual Indian market was established in Santa Fe and talented Indians were encouraged to paint pictures for the first time. In addition, Maria and Julian Martinez of San Ildefonso had just discovered a new technique for the manufacture of attractive black pottery, which was tremendously successful on the commercial market. As a result, many other new pottery styles were perfected, with even stronger emphasis than before on such traits as attractiveness and small size for easy portability in a tourist's suitcase. At the same time several pueblos, notably Zia, Acoma and Santo Domingo, continued to make their classic styles of decorated pottery with nearly as much emphasis on serviceability as on beauty. Sales of pottery through this period remained at a moderate level, high enough to encourage the craftsman, but not outstanding enough to bring riches.

8. THE NATIONAL RECOGNITION PERIOD,

SAN ILDEFONSO AND TESUQUE: *Powhoge black-on-red water jars in the conservative style of the nineteenth century. Circa 1880 and 1840. Height, 27 cm. and 20 cm.*

CHRONOLOGY

1965–PRESENT. During the latter 1960s Indian affairs began to receive prominent national attention, and the result has been an almost incredible increase in demand for fine Indian arts and crafts. Antique rugs, jewelry, pottery and baskets almost disappeared from the market, with the available choice examples commanding many hundreds or even thousands of dollars. The most talented of the modern craftsmen developed and perfected innovative new techniques for the production of artistic wares, and these, too, have commanded enormous prices, with the Indians themselves finally enjoying much of the profit.

In the following chapters, these last four periods, from 1880 to the present, are examined in more detail. The discussion is arranged according to the various areas and villages of the Pueblo Indian world, followed by a discussion of some of the non-pueblo pottery of the other southwestern Indian tribes.

ZIA: *Two superb eighteenth-century vessels, San Pablo Polychrome and Puname Polychrome. Circa 1740 and 1730. Height, 26 cm. and 24 cm.*

COCHITI: *A classic example of Kiua Polychrome at its best, in the form of a storage jar. Circa 1850. Height, 48 cm.*

MODERN PUEBLO POTTERY

PICURIS: *Two fine, light cooking pots, of the type that brought fame to Picuris for their serviceable vessels. Circa 1960. Height, 16 cm. and 25.5 cm.* — Forrest Fenn

THE NORTHERN TIWA PUEBLOS

Taos and Picuris

When James Stevenson visited the famous Pueblo of Taos in about 1880, he found that pottery making had nearly ceased. In the intervening years, there have been no serious attempts at revival of this venerable craft, although a few potters still produce a small output.

Nearby Picuris Pueblo, the most mountainous of all the villages, however, has been justly famous for its fine and serviceable pottery through the modern periods.

Both pueblos manufacture a style of pottery distinctly different from that of all the other ceramics areas, although their Tewa neighbors to the south have produced a ware that imitates the famous pottery, especially from Picuris. The Tiwa style is characterized by a lack of slip and paint, the vessels simply having a well-smoothed exterior, decorated if at all only by sculpturing the clay before it is fired. Typical designs are accomplished by punching rows of dots, by applying ribbons of clay to the surface and building up bumps or knobs.

Especially distinctive is the surface appearance, which glitters from the abundant flakes of mica that are present in the clay. The color is usually like burnished bronze, often mottled by fire clouds to form attractive patterns.

The jars, bowls and pitchers from Picuris Pueblo are especially thin-walled, strong, and well-fired. The rarer examples from Taos are usually heavier and softer-fired.

The Indians and their Spanish neighbors have both treasured Picuris pottery, especially the fine bean pots, said to greatly enhance the flavor of whatever food is cooked in them.

Before using a Picuris bean pot for the first time, it is traditional to prepare the vessel in the following manner. The pot is filled with water with some fat or oil floating on the top, and this is slowly simmered until the water is gone. The purpose is two-fold, to remove the raw earthy smell and taste, and to help seal the pores. Like all southwestern Indian pottery, the vessels are otherwise slightly porous. For water jars, the slight seepage is advantageous, helping to keep the contents cool by evaporation from the outer surface. But for the cooking pots, it is better to seal the pores, which probably also helps cut down on breakage.

The Tewa Indian imitations of Picuris micaceous vessels are respectable pottery in their own right. They are made with typical Tewa area clay, which is almost devoid of micaceous glitter, and then covered with a slip containing abundant mica flakes, thereby producing vessels that closely resemble the northern product. In addition to the distinction in basic clay that can be discerned whenever the pot is chipped, the Tewa vessels can also be distinguished by their lighter or brighter colors, usually heavier weight, and somewhat different forms.

In recent years, some of the best clay beds used by the Picuris potters have been destroyed or damaged by road excavation. In addition, the demand for Picuris pots has decreased because of the easy availability of good, cheap store-bought pans, and because collectors have been more attracted to the flood of decorated styles from the other pueblos. As a result, Picuris pottery is now rarely made, and the village may soon join its picturesque neighbor, Taos, in virtually abandoning the manufacture of ceramics.

PICURIS: *Bean pot and pitcher, both excellent pottery, light in weight and strong. Circa 1920. Height, 13.5 cm. and 17 cm.* — Santa Fe Village

Picuris: *Old style water jar.*
Circa 1800. Height, 32 cm.

SAN JUAN: *Three vessels of San Juan Polychrome by Leonidas Tapia and Bettie Cata. Circa 1973. Height (tallest), 27 cm.* — Bob Ward

THE
TEWA PUEBLOS

IN THE RIO GRANDE VALLEY north of Santa Fe, there are six tiny pueblos whose common bond is the Tewa language, together with a long and distinguished history of contact with the first Europeans in the area and their descendants. Despite the continuous attempts to destroy, replace, or at least influence the Indian traditions, the Europeans were remarkably unsuccessful. Even today the Tewas, like so many of the other Pueblo Indian groups, retain tremendous ties to their ancient culture. The sacred dances and costumes attest to this on numerous occasions each year. Their pottery continued for several centuries to follow exactly the course of evolution that one would have expected if the outsiders never had appeared on the scene.

Two rather different styles of ceramics occur in the Tewa villages, although much exchange of both pots and potters has served to mix the styles somewhat throughout the area. The northern style is traditionally unpainted, whereas the southern Tewa pueblos traditionally painted designs on their pottery.

San Juan

The two northern pueblos have Spanish saints' names, San Juan and Santa Clara. The Indian names for these villages are Oke and Kapo, respectively. The traditional pottery for both is unpainted, being partially red-slipped on tan at San Juan, and black at Santa Clara.

The San Juan Red-on-tan pottery has been the standard style for several centuries at that village. Fine, serviceable pottery was made in the form of both jars and bowls, the latter especially preserving the form that had been standard in the Tewa area since about 1600.

To achieve the red-on-tan color, an oxidizing fire is used. It is very common, however, for imperfect burning of fuel chunks to leave fire clouds on San Juan pottery. Just as at Picuris, these mottled patterns, arranged by chance, are not at all considered blemishes.

Older San Juan vessels usually have no interior red slip, and the red on the outside extends only part way down the surface. On jars, the lower edge of the red area may be marked by a slight depression or groove clear around the pot. On bowls, the red usually covers only the upper exterior, where the surface is concave in vertical profile. The lower edge of the red coincides with the change in form to the convex lower slopes. The classic bowl style has a sharp, angular bend at the place where concave becomes convex, but later bowls from San Juan may have a rounded transition in curvature at this place.

Sometimes the San Juan vessels are fired in a

completely reducing flame, in which case the unslipped areas are dark gray and the red-slipped areas become a polished black color. Such pots can be very difficult to distinguish from the polished black vessels made at Santa Clara Pueblo. As a guide to the distinctions that sometimes can be discerned, the San Juan pots are usually lighter in weight and may have a small amount of very fine micaceous glitter on the unslipped surfaces.

The greatest difficulty in distinguishing the black pots of San Juan from those of Santa Clara is encountered for the unsculptured, rather spherical jars. If the jar is sculptured with bear-paw indentations, then a Santa Clara origin is indicated. Otherwise, the distinction is difficult to make, as both villages produced jars of rather simple form, tall elliptical shape with a slight neck, ranging in size from a few centimeters tall to giant storage jars, some as tall as eighty centimeters.

Bowls from the two villages are more easily identified, as the San Juan style usually retains the classic form described above, whereas the Santa Clara bowls often have a widely flaring, fluted rim.

Jars of more classic form from Santa Clara are also easily distinguished, as they possess both a body that flares from the concave base and a relatively narrow neck that is tall and nearly vertical, surmounted by a flaring rim.

Classic red-on-tan and black pottery styles continue to be made at San Juan until the present

SAN JUAN: *Indian Lady carrying a large water jar in the traditional fashion, photographed by Parkhurst, circa 1920.* — Museum of New Mexico Photo Archives

SAN JUAN: *An unusual double-mouth pitcher of polished black pottery. Circa 1920. Height, 25.5 cm.* — Santa Fe Village

SAN JUAN: *Polychrome jar by Mary R. Cata and polished red bowl by Luteria Atencio. Circa 1975, 1965. Height, 17 cm. and 19.5 cm.*

time, although in recent years the demand for decorated Indian pottery by the tourist and collector market has resulted in the development of some very beautiful new types of San Juan pottery.

One of these is virtually unique to San Juan. It is an incised style, initiated by Mrs. Regina Cata in about 1931. Five centuries earlier, the ancestral Tewa Indians had produced a striking pottery type called Potsuwi'i Incised, but the style was popular for only about fifty years, and rarely made thereafter. From the ancient fragments lying about in nearby ruins, Mrs. Cata conceived of the idea of incising designs in the otherwise undecorated San Juan pottery styles of her day. On the unslipped areas of her pots, she scratched the patterns in simple, straight-line motifs much like those of the ancient type. She then filled the lines with golden micaceous slip, fired the pots in an oxidizing atmosphere, and obtained a very pleasing contrast of textures. The glossy red areas beautifully complement the rough tan incised areas with their golden glitter, and the results have been popular from that day until the present.

Another development at San Juan has been a polychrome style in which the unslipped areas have designs in unpolished red or white clay paint, edged with incised lines. The surfaces near the rim and the base are polished red, which makes an attractive contrast to the unpolished but well-smoothed design areas.

At the present time, there is still much pottery being made at San Juan Pueblo, although less than at Santa Clara or some of the other more productive villages.

Santa Clara

The traditional home of polished black pottery is Santa Clara Pueblo, where that style has been the predominant ceramic trend for nearly three centuries. The most admired of the traditional black Santa Clara pots are the huge storage jars, usually embellished with bear-paw sculpture, the medium-sized water jars with graceful vase-like forms, and the double-spouted wedding vases. Prior to about 1920, these polished black vessels were highly serviceable. The larger ones, used for storage of dried materials, were strong and durable. The medium-size jars, with concave bases for carrying on the head, were excellent for transporting water or milk. But the achievement of this serviceability required higher firing temperatures for the pottery than are used today, when deep black glossy perfection is the goal. The penalty for better firing was that the color of the older pots is usually tinged with dark gray or brown, which, like the fire clouds at San Juan, in no way bothered the Indians. For the best artistic wares, however, the deepest shades of jet black are necessary, requiring somewhat cooler firing.

The change in firing technique accompanied the change in emphasis to commercial sales, following the tremendous success of the polished black wares during the 1920s at nearby San Ildefonso. Both villages found that plain glossy black, or glossy black with dull gray designs (the famous San Ildefonso Black-on-black of Maria and Julian Martinez) was enormously popular with collectors, and the production of these styles has continued with little change to the present day.

In addition, Santa Clara became famous for

SAN JUAN: *A jar and bowl of classic San Juan style, and a modern incised bowl by Rosita Cata. Circa 1900, 1970, 1890. Height, 16 cm., 10 cm. and 18.5 cm.*

the sculpture of pottery figurines, which also are stone-polished to a glossy smoothness and fired to a deep black color. Many different animal forms have been made in sizes ranging from the tiniest miniatures, one or two centimeters in length, up to as much as thirty centimeters long. Recent variations leave parts of the surface unpolished, giving an effective contrast in textures.

Sometimes the larger bowls and jars are also carved. The bear-paw sculpture has already been mentioned. This five-toed figure appears as an indentation to the otherwise smooth surface, and is usually polished. Another popular style of carving leaves the indentations unpolished, from which the polished relief contrasts with great effectiveness. Geometric figures predominate, but Avanyu (the plumed serpent with lightning tongue) is also commonly depicted.

As at all the other pottery-making pueblos, the general trend during this commercially-oriented period has been towards making smaller vessels and ceramic sculpture, and to develop new forms such as ashtrays and candlesticks. At Santa Clara, however, there are still a few potters capable and willing to make very large vessels. Margaret Tafoya usually makes one huge black storage jar each year, a real *tour de force* requiring months of careful drying of the clay body, many tedious hours of polishing to achieve the incredibly beautiful surface, and a most careful firing to achieve uniform deep black color and avoid cracking the vessel. At present, no other potter from any village will attempt such a feat, although some at Santa Clara and elsewhere still occasionally produce vessels up to two-thirds the size of Mrs. Tafoya's.

More frequently than at San Ildefonso, the Santa Clara potters also have produced red pottery for the last half century. The technique is identical to that of the black pottery style except for the firing, which is accomplished with a good draft of air to produce an oxidizing atmosphere. One Santa Clara potter, the famous Mrs. Severa Tafoya, once told me that she avoided making red pottery because a dealer complained that the vessels faded with time. The dealer's complaint, however, is nonsense, as the earth colors are entirely permanent.

Often the Santa Clara red wares have designs painted in shades of pink, gray, yellow and other warm colors. In contrast to the San Juan painted designs, which are applied to the unpolished basic clay and bordered by incised lines, the Santa Clara decorations are usually painted directly onto the polished slip.

One family, Lela and Van Gutierrez, developed a variant in which intricate designs in many different pastel shades of matte paint are applied to a light tan background. The popularity of this style has been tremendous, and it is still continued by Margaret and Luther, the descendants of the inventors, but has not been taken up by any other of the Santa Clara potters.

A very recent style of carving at Santa Clara Pueblo has also proved to be popular. In this case the very delicate carvings are incised into the polished surface of the vessel, sometimes in such a way as to produce a truly three-dimensional sculpture. Many of the most exquisite of these art works are quite small, being easily held in the palm of the hand. They may be all black or all red in color, or they may be mottled. The latter have carefully controlled areas of both black and tan or brick red, achieved by special firing techniques requiring carefully controlled and directed flames.

Regarding the famous Santa Clara bear paw design, many people wonder about its history and significance. The earliest examples of the figure apparently date from the middle of the nineteenth century. Several Santa Clara potters have described for me the origin of the bear paw. I like the following version:

"The summer weather was hot and dry. The crops were wilting, the people thirsty. The river carried no water. Each day the people of the village became more worried. The dance for rain was held, and the wisest elders called upon the spirits for relief. And then, when desperation was becoming most intense, a shout was heard. Come see, a bear is coming to the village. Sure enough, down through the canyon from the mountains came a wise old bear, alone and unafraid. Although the people were very hungry, the bear should not be killed. The circumstances were not proper, and sacred preparations for a hunt had not been made. So everyone simply watched and waited as the bear, with deliberate intention, walked on through the village. No one could understand, except the eldest wise man. He called the people all together and told them the bear commanded that they follow him. So slowly did he move, it seemed forever as he ambled over past the mesa of departed spirits and started up a small arroyo back towards the mountains. Finally, just as Tan Tsendo, the sun, was setting, and the valley back behind them turned blood red, the journey ended. The bear had led them to a little spring of cool, fresh water. No one had found this spot before, because the thirsty sands consumed the moisture before it could get very far. The bear continued on his way. The village had been saved."

The legend ends by saying that after that, the bear should be remembered with his paw print on all the vessels made at Santa Clara, so that even today this graceful emblem occurs often, usually in sets of three or four around the upper body of a jar.

The peculiar vessel form called a wedding jar is also sometimes considered to be a Santa Clara specialty, but examples are made at most of the other pueblos. The classic form is constructed with a nearly spherical body from which rise two nearly cylindrical necks, joined by a handle, and spouted away from each other. At one time it was

SANTA CLARA: *Polychrome vessels by Lela Guiterrez with decorations by Luther, Van and Luther. Circa 1960. Height (tallest), 26 cm.*

thought that this form is only an innovation to catch the tourist's eye, but the style actually has ancient antecedents, to be found in double-spouted vessels made in Peru nearly two thousand years ago. Descendant forms throughout middle America show up in the pueblo area at about the time of William the Conqueror in England, and rare examples were made during the next four or five centuries, and again commencing in the late nineteenth century, probably inspired by surviving earlier vessels. The ancient purpose is, of course, lost in antiquity, but observations of recent use at Santa Clara show its importance in traditional Indian wedding ceremonies. A drink from each side by bride and groom occurs at the most solemn moment of the sacred celebration. At other pueblos drinking from a wedding vase may be replaced by an exchange of necklaces, and Santa Clara may be the only village still using the wedding vase for true ceremonial purposes.

SANTA CLARA: *A huge storage jar with bear-paw designs, made by Mrs. Naranjo. Circa 1930. Height, 57.5 cm.*

SANTA CLARA: *Water jar with bear-paw designs and a wedding vase, both made to be used. Circa 1900. Height, 31.5 cm. and 26 cm.*

SANTA CLARA: *Wedding vase and sugar bowl, the latter perhaps from San Juan. Circa 1925. Height, 14 cm. and 10 cm.* — Santa Fe Village

SANTA CLARA: *Very large wedding vase of carved black pottery by Margaret Tafoya. Circa 1960. Height, 49 cm.*

SANTA CLARA: *Horse figure of polished black pottery made by Margaret Naranjo. Circa 1950. Length, 22 cm.* — Santa Fe Village

SANTA CLARA

SANTA CLARA: *Carved jar with polished red and rough tan by Joseph Lonewolf. Circa 1975. Height, 9 cm.* — Forrest Fenn

SANTA CLARA: *Carved plate with polished red and rough tan by Grace Medicine Flower. Circa 1975. Diameter, 31 cm.* — Forrest Fenn

SANTA CLARA: *Polychrome bowl and plate by Belen Tapia, and a carved black bowl by Legoria. Circa 1960. Height, 18 cm.; diameter, 26 cm.; height, 20 cm.*

SANTA CLARA: *These polished black pottery animals are a Santa Clara specialty. Circa 1950. Height (tallest), 10 cm.*

SANTA CLARA: *Numerous tiny pottery vessels by Art Cody. Circa 1975. Height, 1.5 cm. to 9.5 cm.* — Bob Ward

San Ildefonso

San Ildefonso Pueblo, with the Indian name of Powhoge, has in recent years been one of the most famous of all the pottery-making villages. As at the other three southern Tewa pueblos, the traditional pottery style for centuries was a polychrome ware, with black decorations in vegetal paint and red derived from a clay slip.

Until 1880, the red color was used in the designs themselves only rarely (mainly on Ogapoge Polychrome, a seldom encountered pottery type of the early eighteenth century). Instead, from 1760–1880 the red was confined to the top of the rim and in a narrow band just below the white slipped design area. During this period, the pottery type, called Powhoge Polychrome, was popular and widely traded, and made at several villages besides San Ildefonso. It also influenced the development of several descendant pottery types at the nearby pueblos of Nambe, Pojoaque and Tesuque, and even at the more distant Keres-speaking pueblos of Santo Domingo and Cochiti.

Indeed, the resulting style at the Keres pueblos, called Kiua Polychrome, strongly resembles the older Powhoge Polychrome, and was made for much longer than the Tewa type. As a result, many people have tended to forget the older Powhoge Polychrome, and to assign any such vessels that come to light a Santo Domingo or Cochiti origin. There are, however, some very clear distinctions. One of the most useful is the black rim color on Kiua Polychrome, instead of the red on Powhoge Polychrome. Other technical details aid in the differentiation, which is discussed further in the section on Santo Domingo.

In 1880, James Stevenson wrote about his extensive visits to the pueblos of New Mexico. Concerning San Ildefonso, he stated that the people "have almost abandoned the manufacture of pottery, that in use by them at the present time being mostly obtained from neighboring tribes." Nevertheless, he obtained a rather large collection of vessels there, seventeen bowls, three water jars and one large storage jar, all currently stored in the United States National Museum. Apparently all were decorated with black designs on cream, with no red in the decorations.

Two years later the noted anthropologist, Adolph Bandelier, wrote in his journal, "I examined the recent pottery of San Ildefonso. It is red and black, rather handsome. Cochiti also is beginning to paint its pottery red."

What Stevenson had missed, Bandelier observed, namely the birth of a pottery-making revival at San Ildefonso that was to propel that tiny village into international prominence as a center for manufacture of beautiful pottery.

The impetus was the coming of the railroad to New Mexico, with a flood of eager and curious Easterners, which initiated a flurry of new activity in Indian arts and crafts. San Ildefonso Polychrome, dating from about 1880, is a result. After about 1830, San Ildefonso had made very little of its pottery, much being imported from nearby pueblos, or obtained in trade from the newly opened Santa Fe Trail. But the revival in 1880 changed all that completely. Many of the San Ildefonso residents began learning the craft from the older women who still knew the techniques, and started producing new styles designed to catch the fancy of the tourists. In particular, they returned to the more classic vase-like forms that had been perpetuated at Santa Clara, and also started using red in the designs. To avoid fire-cloud blemishes, the pots were sometimes fired in a more easily controlled, relatively cool fire, and accordingly are softer and less serviceable. But for market appeal this new style of pottery was such a success that large numbers were produced over a relatively few years.

At its finest, San Ildefonso Polychrome is a superbly handsome pottery type. In every respect it carries on all of the native traditions for construction materials, technique of manufacture, design layout and motifs, and emphasis on quality of the finished product. In the hands of Martina and Florentino Montoya at the turn of the century, the craft became truly an art. Those gifted potters produced some magnificent vessels, but their works are so rarely encountered now that their names are almost forgotten.

One legacy of the Montoyas to San Ildefonso pottery making was the introduction of Cochiti slip in about 1907. Cochiti slip is white like the native slip used previously at San Ildefonso, but it is amenable to smoothing or polishing by a rag, instead of by the more tedious process of stone stroking required for the native slip. Although the Montoyas themselves mostly worked with native slip, the other village potters turned almost exclusively to the new material to produce a pottery type we call Tunyo Polychrome. This last of the San Ildefonso white-slip polychrome pottery types is distinguished by its more grainy, striated slip, and for vessels after about 1955, by the more intense colors of the painted designs. Since the introduction of Cochiti slip, the stone-polished native slip has not been used on pottery seen by the public, but has been reserved instead only for special-purpose vessels used in the village.

The most famous of all Pueblo Indian potters, Maria Martinez, commenced her craft just after the introduction of Cochiti slip, and almost all of her earliest vessels were finished with this material. Even from the start, Maria's standards of excellence were visible. We can distinguish these early products of her career by their relatively thin walls, light weight, hard firing and by the gracefulness of form and excellence of design. A strongly outflaring jar rim is especially characteristic of Maria's work. Although Maria has never painted the designs on her pottery, she always insisted on collaborating only with the most talented of the village artists. In particular, her husband, Julian, was exceptionally skillful and imaginative, and produced easily recognizable patterns of great precision and artistic balance. When Julian was away, for example, working with the anthropologists excavating the ruins of his ancestors' villages, then Maria would choose her sister, Maximiliana, or her cousin, Alfredo Montoya, to paint the designs. Sometimes Maximiliana's husband, Crescencio Martinez, also decorated Maria's pottery.

Each of these artists had styles that we can recognize today, thanks to the memory of Maria and her talented family, who have willingly related their knowledge of this early part of the twentieth century. The decorative patterns of Maximiliana are recognized by their relative boldness and simplicity. She apparently preferred large geometrical figures, which she painted with care. Alfredo liked to paint fancy birds and insects, almost always in association with flowers. He often would also paint curved or angular meandering red lines edged with black in a distinctive style used previously by Florentino Montoya. Alfredo's design execution is somewhat less precise than that of Maximiliana, but is more delicate, ornate and imaginative. Julian's style is the most precise, delicate and imaginative of all. The variety of his patterns seems almost endless, ranging from very simple geometric patterns to the most complex, incorporating motifs from throughout the Pueblo world. When he depicts birds, they are drawn with grace and beauty, sometimes in very naturalistic form and sometimes highly stylized, but always simpler, less ornate or fancy, than those of Alfredo, and never in association with flowers. Crescencio also preferred simpler bird figures, much like those of Julian.

Despite the excellent work of the more talented potters, the popularity of San Ildefonso Polychrome did not persist, and Tunyo Polychrome apparently never caught the fancy of tourists or collectors until the late revival of its manufacture by Maria's son, Popovi Da, in about 1956. The enthusiasm of dealers and collectors in the period 1900–1920 probably was soured in part by the production of numerous rather degenerate examples, and the Indians' enthusiasm was abated by the decrease in both market and price. The effects of World War I may also have been appreciable. Maria remembers that even the finest examples often sold for no more than twenty-five cents, which was small wages indeed for the many hours required in the construction of each vase.

It is an irony of circumstances that the best of these old vessels now command prices of many thousands of dollars, and even the poorest cannot be obtained for less than several hundred.

A somewhat different style concurrent with San Ildefonso Polychrome was San Ildefonso Black-on-red, made principally by Dominguita Pino and her daughter, Tonita Roybal. The forms of this handsome pottery type are like those of San Ildefonso and Tunyo Polychromes. The designs are painted in black guaco over a completely red surface. The last vessels of this style were made in the 1920s.

At the end of World War I there arose at San Ildefonso yet another style of pottery, in this case so successful in its appeal to the commercial market that it continues unabated to the present day. Discovered shortly before 1920 by Maria and Julian Martinez, the style is called San Ildefonso Black-on-black. Taking the old idea for plain black pottery, this couple introduced two changes. For one, they found that by painting a mineral pigment over the polished surface before firing, the final result would have a beautiful dull-dark-gray-on-polished-black appearance. The second discovery was a refinement in the technique for reduced firing, which produced a much deeper, more uniform black color. The results were sensational! Instead of taking home a tourist trinket, the visitor to New Mexico could take with him a sophisticated piece of artistry that would fit into the decor of even the most modern New York apartment.

In the early days of this matte-paint-on-polished-surface pottery, some vessels were fired in an oxidizing atmosphere, producing pinkish matte decorations on the polished red surface. It was the black-on-black style, however, that was always more popular, so that the oxidized examples are rarely produced any longer.

The success of this new style was so great that the other potters of San Ildefonso wanted to learn the secret. Although the technique was soon shared, both among the Martinez neighbors and to the craftsmen of nearby Santa Clara, it was Maria and Julian and their daughter-in-law, Santana, who remained the master potters of this style. Through the years, one added feature has even further enhanced the beauty of the Martinez family output, the discovery of a technique for giving a silvery gun-metal luster to the polished black surfaces, which no other potters have been able to duplicate. In recent years, Maria's sister, Clara, has accomplished much of the beautiful polishing.

The earliest of the black-on-black pots produced by Maria and Julian were unsigned. As with the previous polychrome wares, no one ever thought that a signature would be of interest or value. On the first of these unsigned black pots, only that part of the black surface was polished where the design was to show, and the matte paint was applied over the rest. Soon they discovered that it was both easier and nicer looking to polish the entire surface and apply the matte paint to a much more restricted area. A frequent pattern used by Julian is the Avanyu, a serpent with a plume or horn on its head. The serpent itself was always polished, with the surrounding being matte. The earliest Avanyus had a very simple plume; later ones were embellished with a hand-like figure with triangular fingers on the tip of the plume. Starting about 1923, Maria sometimes signed her pottery on the bottom by means of a smooth stone pressed into the clay. The earliest signature was simply "Marie" but by around 1925 or a little later she wrote "Marie & Julian," which persisted until Julian's death in 1943.

Polychrome pottery made by the couple during the 1920s was also occasionally signed in paint with Maria's Indian name, "Poh've'ka." In 1922, an unsigned polychrome bowl won second prize at the Santa Fe Indian fair. The vessel is in rectangular form, with a stair-step terrace at each end. It is decorated with guaco paint, using designs that Julian copied from an old Tesuque bowl. By 1925, the couple was experimenting with a new paint that left a slightly purple tinge to the black. They also were making jars that are black-on-red on the upper part and polychrome on the lower part. One has the signature, Poh've'ka, showing quite prominently in the design area, and a bowl with similar exterior designs has that same signature on an otherwise completely plain white interior.

After Julian's death, Maria's daughter-in-law, Santana Martinez, collaborated in the design work, and such pots are signed "Marie & Santana" until about 1948 or 1950, and "Maria & Santana" thereafter. Commencing in 1956, Maria also collaborated with her son, who always used his Indian name, Popovi Da, signing such pots "Maria Popovi." After Po's death in 1971, Maria has mainly worked with Santana, who also makes many fine pots of her own. Although her output has been quite small in these recent years, Maria's hands are strong and her eyes, following cataract removal, are sharp. In this most recent period, when she signs an old polychrome pot that she recognizes, Maria may use any of a variety of signatures, including "Maria Povika Julian," adding her husband's name if he was the painter of designs on the vessel.

One popular variation of the polished black style has the designs carved into the surface. Rose Gonzales has been considered the most skillful and artistic of the pottery carvers at San Ildefonso,

SAN ILDEFONSO: *Two polychrome vessels. Left, a jar made by Maria Martinez and signed with her Indian name, Poh've'ka; right, a terraced bowl in the style of a ceremonial vessel. Circa 1925. Height, 21 cm. and 17.5 cm.* — Museum of New Mexico 18798/12 and 36005/12

where the style has not been so widely used as at nearby Santa Clara.

During the most recent years, there have been several directions of somewhat more innovative experimentation. Delicate incising and carving of the black or red polished surface is now seen, in addition to the deeper and bolder carving in the work of Rose Gonzales. New materials have been introduced, for example, polished turquoise nuggets are sometimes mounted onto the polished surface, and lids are made of silver or jet, to produce elaborate creations. Some of these have been very skillfully constructed and command prices above a thousand dollars each.

Another direction of experimentation has been with new pigments of various sorts, painted onto polished backgrounds of black, red or white color. The design lines thus exhibit startling new hues, including green, which had last been seen on pueblo pottery in some of the rare prehistoric mineral glazes at Acoma Pueblo.

At San Ildefonso, as at a few of the other villages, pottery making continues to be a major industry, and some of the best craftsmen are realizing large financial gain from the sale of their wares. Seemingly going through a slight decline in the period 1955–1965, the craft has experienced an incredible revival during the last decade, sparked by a national interest in fine Indian-made products, and San Ildefonso is playing a prominent part in producing the pottery that has made this renewed interest possible.

SAN ILDEFONSO: *Black-on-red bowl and jar by Tonita Roybal. Circa 1920. Diameter, 20.5 cm.; height, 19.5 cm.* — Museum of New Mexico 18751/12 and 11245/12

SAN ILDEFONSO: *Juan Cruz Roybal and his wife, Tonita, photographed by Parkhurst in about 1925.* — Museum of New Mexico Photo Archives

SAN ILDEFONSO: *Tunyo Polychrome jar made by Maria Martinez and decorated by Alfredo Montoya. Circa 1910. Height, 21.5 cm.* — Santa Fe Village

SAN ILDEFONSO: *Tunyo Polychrome storage jar with lid. Circa 1905. Height 39 cm.* — Bob Ward

SAN ILDEFONSO: *Tunyo Polychrome water jar made by Maria Martinez and decorated by her sister, Maximiliana. Maria holds the jar on her head in a 1975 photograph. Circa 1910. Height, 26 cm.* — John Rivenburgh

SAN ILDEFONSO: *Polychrome jar made for domestic use and showing the effect of much service. Circa 1890. Height, 27 cm.*

SAN ILDEFONSO: *A fine water jar showing horizontal stone-polishing marks. Circa 1900. Height, 19 cm.* — Bob Ward

SAN ILDEFONSO: *Polished black pottery box by Tony Da. Circa 1965. Width, 16 cm.*

SAN ILDEFONSO: *Black-on-black feather plate by Santana and Adam Martinez. Circa 1960. Diameter, 24 cm.*

SAN ILDEFONSO: *Tan-on-red and black-on-black vessels by Maria Martinez. Left, decorated by Maria's son, Popovi Da; right, by Maria's husband, Julian. Circa 1955, 1922. Height, 22 cm. and 18.5 cm.*

SAN ILDEFONSO: *A magnificent example of San Ildefonso Polychrome in the form of a sacred ceremonial jar. Circa 1900. Height, 27 cm.*

SAN ILDEFONSO: *Tunyo Polychrome water jar made by Maria Martinez and decorated by her husband, Julian. Circa 1910. Height, 28.5 cm.* — Forrest Fenn

SAN ILDEFONSO: *Polychrome storage jar with unusual face design. Circa 1900. Height, 42.5 cm.*

Nambe and Pojoaque

Neither of these pueblos produces a significant amount of pottery at the present time. Pojoaque, whose pueblo entity was nearly lost in the earlier years of this century, had a ceramics history apparently like that of nearby Nambe, for which the evolution of pottery styles is much better known.

Until about 1830, Nambe was a major center for the production of a type of pottery much like Powhoge Polychrome. Distinguished by the occasional large mica flakes in its clay, by the relatively poor quality of its slip, and by some distinctive design styles, the type is called Nambe Polychrome.

There is considerable evidence to indicate that Nambe Polychrome was exported to many of the surrounding Indian villages, to the Spanish homes in Santa Fe, and to as far as Pecos Pueblo. Whole vessels are extremely rare today; I know of only four, but many thousands of fragments have been available for study, mostly from the vicinity of the village itself.

With the opening of trade routes to the east in the 1820s the demand for decorated pottery decreased markedly, and Nambe responded by ceasing the manufacture of its famous polychrome

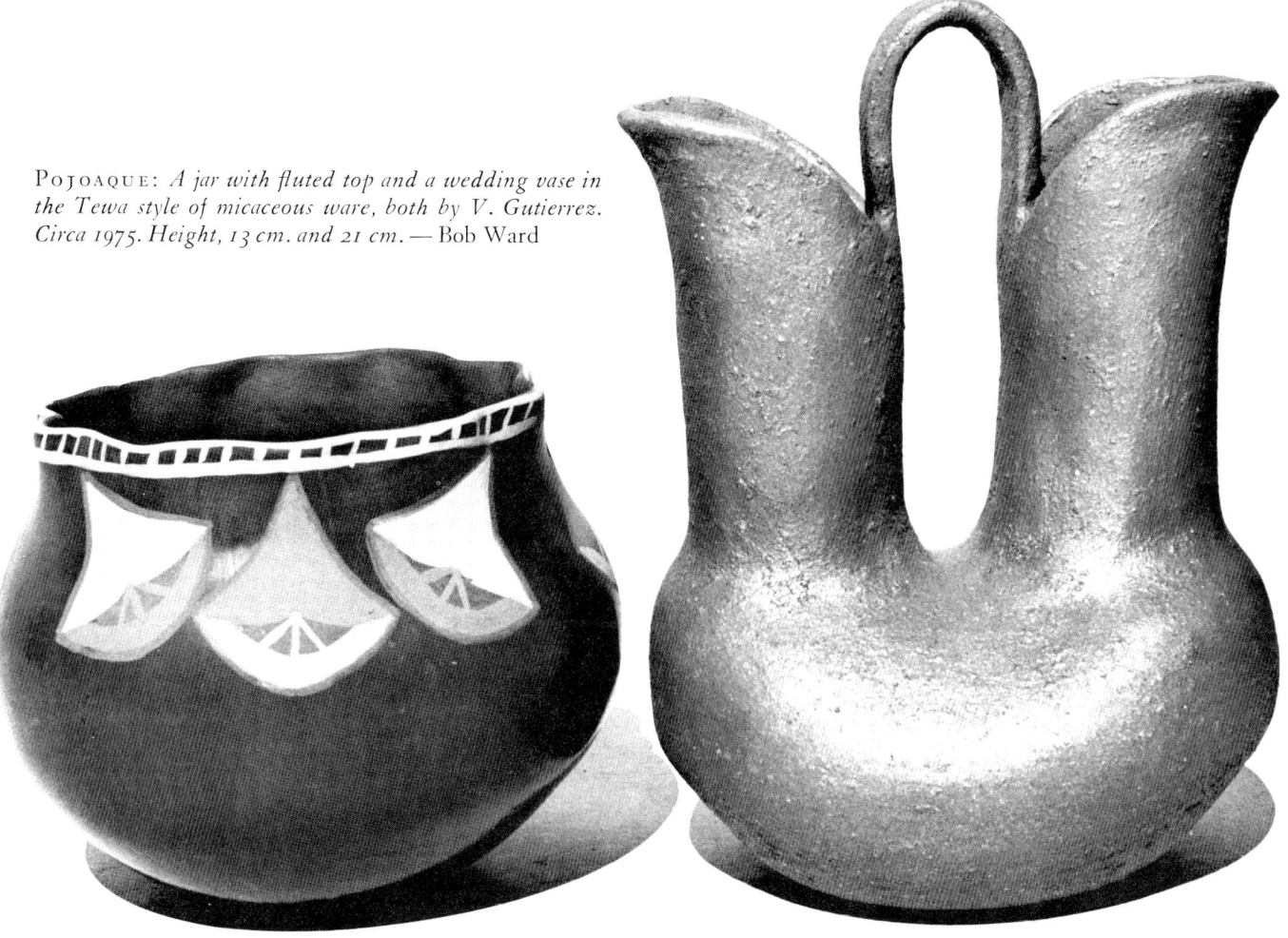

POJOAQUE: *A jar with fluted top and a wedding vase in the Tewa style of micaceous ware, both by V. Gutierrez. Circa 1975. Height, 13 cm. and 21 cm.* — Bob Ward

style. The village had been making polished red or black pottery and various types of utility wares, however, and these continued unabated for at least another century. Even today, the older residents of surrounding villages tell of Nambe traders exporting their pottery until as late as 1900. The Nambe Indians themselves still remember some of the potters, the last of whom died only a few years ago.

Polished black bowls and jars from Nambe are so similar to the ones from Santa Clara that only a close technical analysis can distinguish the pueblo of origin. The polished red wares are somewhat more distinctive, again differentiated from the products of other pueblos principally through the presence of the occasional large mica flakes that wash into their clay beds from the pre-Cambrian rocks nearby.

Until as late as the 1940s the Nambe potters were the principal makers of the pottery type that mimics the micaceous wares of Picuris and Taos. In contrast to the usual pots from Nambe, in which the distinctive flakes of mica are relatively rare and accidental, this deliberately micaceous style has a slip that is abundantly filled with glitter. To distinguish these pots from the Picuris and Taos products, it is usually necessary to see into the layers of clay below the slip, where the clay is of the usual Nambe type. In addition, the Nambe vessels are often lighter in color and heavier in weight.

NAMBE: *Two vessels showing the last of the Nambe pottery styles. Left, polished black; right, polished brown by Josefita Anaya. Circa 1920, 1950. Diameter, 28 cm. and 19 cm.* — Museum of New Mexico 45538/12 and 45537/12

POJOAQUE: *Two beautiful jars in the style of eighteenth-century Pojoaque Polychrome, made by Joe and Thelma Talachy. Circa 1975. Height, 19 cm.* — Museum of New Mexico

Tesuque

The ceramics from Tesuque have enjoyed a long and distinguished history, somewhat clouded by the poster-paint styles introduced in the 1920s.

The finest examples of Powhoge Polychrome were made at Tesuque in a sequence of style from which Tesuque Polychrome evolved in about 1830.

Tesuque Polychrome differs from its ancestral type principally in the characteristic designs employed to decorate the surface. The brilliant exuberance of this style is especially apparent in the work of one unknown potter whose principal output appears to have been during the 1880s. This gifted craftsman made many vessels, some of them very large storage jars, and decorated them with patterns so distinctive that they serve almost as a signature.

While Tesuque Polychrome continued to be made until somewhat after 1900, it was joined in the late 1800s by a companion style called Tatunque Polychrome, distinguished by the use of red in the designs. In contrast to the contemporary San Ildefonso Polychrome, in which the design-area red is almost invariably edged with black, the Tesuque type usually has some part of the red that is isolated, that is, not edged with black lines.

Late examples of Tatunque Polychrome have the startling innovation of incorporating a very pale blue pigment into the designs. Some of these vessels are otherwise completely typical of good-quality Tesuque Polychrome, and it is not certain whether the blue pigment was added to such vessels after firing, or was actually fired into the slip.

At some time around 1910, a new type of slip began to see service on Tesuque pottery. The material is like a satiny cream, and gives a uniquely Tesuque appearance to the pots. Decorations were accomplished by pale pink and blue pigments. Some of these vessels are quite handsome indeed, well made, nicely polished and hard fired. Others, especially the very small examples

TESUQUE: *A sacred ceremonial jar with figures of the plumed serpent, clouds, feathers and stars, obtained from Nambe Pueblo. Circa 1890. Height, 29 cm.*

made for sale to tourists in nearby Santa Fe, are extremely crude in all respects. The style apparently did not last long, being replaced in the 1920s by the introduction of the more gaudy poster-paint pottery. In this new technique the pottery piece was formed, smoothed, fired, all before any designs were applied. The patterns were then painted in a dazzling display of bright colors, employing both Indian and pseudo-Indian motifs. For the unwary, the purchase of such pottery could lead to disillusionment, for any brush with dampness results in smearing of the paint.

Other pueblos have also adopted one or another version of the commercial-pigment styles, in recent years sometimes hiding the fact by spraying the whole surface with an aerosol fixative.

Occasionally a Tesuque potter attempts to return to the ceramics styles of the previous century. Priscilla Vigil made some attractive vessels with fired-on guaco paint during the 1950s, but finding their construction quite time consuming, and get-ting very little response from prospective purchasers, she soon abandoned the effort.

Lorencita Pino has also recently produced a few vessels with guaco paint on Cochiti slip. Several of these are quite large, and she has received encouragement from both anthropologists and collectors. Her more famous style, however, is the micaceous-slipped pottery that she makes in the Tewa version of Picuris-Taos wares. Mrs. Pino often sculpts her micaceous pots into strange shapes, including some with human faces.

During this century, Tesuque potters have often produced a particularly characteristic sculpture in human form, called the "rain god." The seated figure with legs thrust out in front, holds a pot in its lap, and may be decorated in any of a variety of styles, including the simple micaceous-slip finish that mimics the pottery of Picuris. These figures have no historical or religious significance, being produced entirely for the tourist and collector's market.

TESUQUE: *Black-on-red jar with lid. Circa 1890. Height, 27 cm.* — Museum of New Mexico 19342/12

TESUQUE: *Revival-style jar by Priscilla Vigil, and decorative jar of Tatungue Polychrome. Circa 1960 and 1890. Height, 12.5 and 20 cm.*

TESUQUE: *Four poster-paint items of pottery. The left rain god and wedding vase are circa 1950. The right-most rain god is circa 1920, before the swastika became an unpopular symbol of Nazi Germany. Rain-god height, 17 cm.*

TESUQUE: *A superb water jar of Tatungue Polychrome. Circa 1890. Height, 29 cm.* — Forrest Fenn

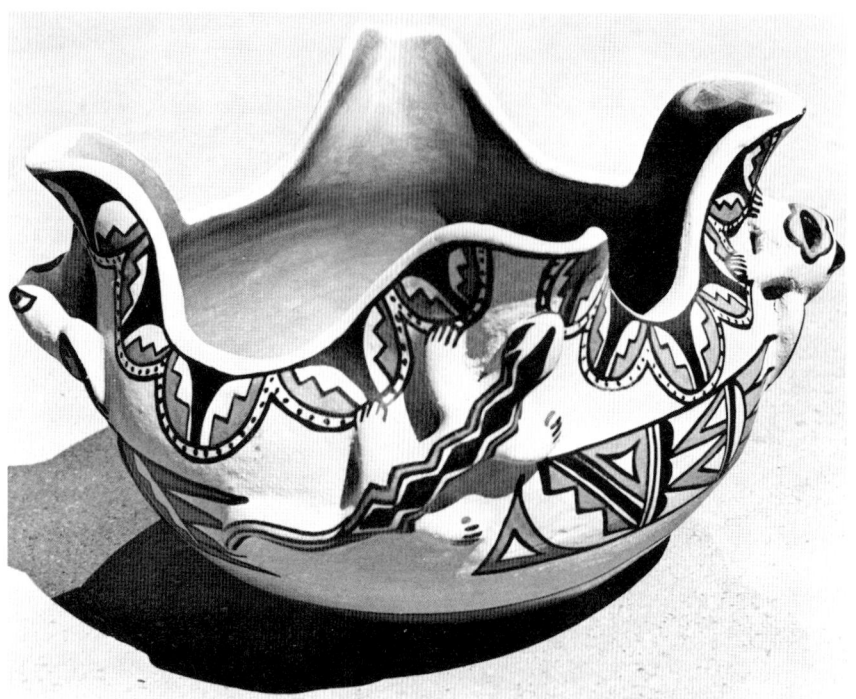

TESUQUE: *Decorative bowl with sculptured lizards and frogs, by Lorencita Pino. Circa 1975. Height, 10 cm.* — Al Packard

TESUQUE: *Highly polished water jar with fluted rim. Circa 1920. Height, 14 cm.* — Bob Ward

TESUQUE

TESUQUE: *Two modern bowls with old Tesuque designs by Lorencita Pino. Circa 1975. Diameter, 27 cm.* — Museum of New Mexico

TESUQUE: *A large pottery vessel with the form and sacred designs of a ceremonial bowl. Circa 1920. Height, 23.5 cm.* — Ford Ruthling

TESUQUE: *Large bowl with Cochiti slip. Circa 1915. Height, 25 cm.* — Santa Fe Village

COCHITI: *Three figurines. Left, by Seferina Sevenna; middle and right, by Helen Cordero. Circa 1890, 1970 and 1970. Height (tallest), 43 cm.* — Forrest Fenn

THE NORTHEAST KERES PUEBLOS

ALONG THE RIO GRANDE between Santa Fe and Albuquerque there are three pueblos at which the Keres language is spoken, two of them with pottery traditions that after about 1760 became quite similar to those of the Tewa-speaking pueblos north of Santa Fe. Cochiti, Santo Domingo, and San Felipe are descendant in part from ancestral homes in the nearby cliffs of the Jemez Mountains, where the traditional prehistoric decorated pottery was painted with glazing minerals.

After the Pueblo Indian revolt in 1680 and the reconquest by DeVargas in 1692 and 1694, there was a period of great upheaval, and the glaze-ware traditions, among other things, were somehow lost in the shuffle. Pueblo populations were uprooted, moved about, intermingled and from the chaos new village localities were settled, new mixtures of influences were felt and new styles of pottery making emerged. Some pueblos, like San Felipe, ceased entirely the manufacture of decorated pottery. Others established new traditions for themselves, in both instances turning to the use of guaco paint for designs much like those of their Tewa tutors.

San Felipe

With cultural ties closer to those of Santa Ana than Santo Domingo, the San Felipe Indians since 1700 have produced polished red pottery with river-washed sand for temper, much like the plain pottery of Santa Ana and Isleta. They have also made some of their own utility wares. For decorated pottery, however, San Felipe Pueblo has relied on several of the other villages, especially Zia and Cochiti. Twenty years ago, the visitor to

SAN FELIPE: *A problematical water jar with Cochiti designs on a clay that suggests San Felipe origin. Circa 1840. Height, 28 cm.*

SAN FELIPE / SANTO DOMINGO

San Felipe could see many fine old vessels, some still in use, which had been obtained in trade from other pueblos. At that time the Pueblo Council forbade the Indians to sell or trade these venerable old pots to outsiders. Through the 1950s, however, the regulation gradually weakened, and several Santa Fe traders obtained beautiful old pottery for a few years from San Felipe, until there was little remaining in the village.

In recent years there has been sporadic experimentation with decorated pottery making, but the trends have not become well-established or persistent enough to constitute a revival of the craft, and none of the results so far have found significant appeal in the commercial markets.

SAN FELIPE: *Polished red bowl of classic San Felipe style, and polychrome jar with prominent ceremonial break. Circa 1940. Diameter, 18.5 cm.; height, 23.5 cm.* — Museum of New Mexico 45533/12 and 7782/12

Santo Domingo

The Indian name for this large, thriving, and very conservative pueblo is Kiua. Famous for its jewelry making, the pueblo is also well known for the trading habits of its residents. A typical home may have Navajo rugs on the walls, pottery from the Hopi and Acoma Pueblos on its shelves (but never from nearby Cochiti) and a large inventory of jewelry-making equipment, all obtained in trade from other Indians or from the suppliers in Santa Fe and Albuquerque. Anything of quality that one may propose for trade is eagerly considered by the residents of Santo Domingo Pueblo.

Here is the traditional home of the pottery type, Kiua Polychrome, the first of a line of new styles developed during the 1700s. The earliest examples of Kiua Polychrome evolved from the same influences that were leading to Powhoge Polychrome in the neighboring Tewa Pueblos. But already in 1770 there were noticeable differences between the two types, especially in the materials used for their construction. Kiua Polychrome has much more crushed crystalline rock for its tempering material, and the slip is a different type of fine clay, which can be polished with a rag, in contrast to the native slip of the Tewas which always shows the stroke marks from the required polishing stones.

At first the makers of Kiua Polychrome painted the rim tops of their vessels red, just as on Powhoge Polychrome. The early vessels with this trait, however, are very rare. After about 1800 the rim tops were painted black, a canon that persists to the present day. Another minor but persistent difference is in the nature of the red band between the unslipped basal surface and the white-slipped area for decoration. On Powhoge Polychrome, the band is narrow (usually around a centimeter in width) and formed of a hard, relatively thick, dark red material. On Kiua Polychrome, the band is usually at least twice as wide, and formed of a softer, thinner, more orange-colored material.

During the earliest period the designs on Kiua Polychrome were quite similar to those of Powhoge Polychrome. Soon, however, the Keres potters began to develop a distinctive decorative style of their own. At Santo Domingo, this was formed of heavy, bold, geometric patterns, whereas the Cochiti style became fussier, more delicate in nature.

With typical conservatism for Santo Domingo, the style of Kiua Polychrome made there remained almost unchanged for over a century, and some potters still make vessels that are virtually indistinguishable from those that were made five generations ago. At their finest the vessels are very beautiful, well made, and decorated in vegetal-paint designs that are strong and bold.

In the late 1880s, some of the Santo Domingo potters began to experiment with innovative features such as the use of red in the designs, new layouts for the field of design, and new forms, especially for their jars. These new features combine to define a type called Santo Domingo Polychrome. In addition to the use of red in the designs, the appearance was also changed by the use of new motifs such as birds and flowers, but virtually never any mammal forms, and especially never any humans. Also excluded was the use of sacred symbols such as clouds, rain, lightning, serpents, and water creatures. Indeed, the presence of some of these symbols on the secular pottery at nearby Cochiti must have been very shocking to the conservative residents of Santo Domingo, and may help explain why no Cochiti pottery is to be seen in the Santo Domingo homes.

Whereas Kiua Polychrome designs are virtually always split into a set of rectangular panels around the vessel, the designs of Santo Domingo Polychrome are usually not framed by panel lines, being simply bounded above and below by the usual encircling double-line sets, which as in Kiua Polychrome, are broken at some place by a slight gap (the so-called ceremonial break). A distinctive feature in form for Santo Domingo Polychrome is the somewhat taller, narrower shape of the jars. In the 1920s a variety of other form variants also appeared, mainly in response to the market for small souvenir pieces. Most of these vessels are small bowls, some with handles or fluted rims, usually decorated with big, bold flowers and leaves. Seldom are they well made. Another briefly occurring style in the early years of this century employed geometric designs in black and red polygons covering nearly all available area of the vessel.

A much less traditional variant also has been made at Santo Domingo since about 1930, in which the surface is polished black or red, with mineral or commercial paints used for designs, often painted after the pot was fired.

The tradition for a red band below the design area, mentioned as such an invariable feature for Kiua Polychrome, is also present on some vessels of Santo Domingo Polychrome, but this tradition, too, was lost by almost all potters during the 1920s. Thereafter, with rare exceptions the underbody has been slipped an allover red color. At the other Rio Grande pueblos where red banding was still the rule by 1900 (Zia, Santa Ana, Cochiti, Tesuque, San Ildefonso), the tradition also died during the period 1915–1930, serving as a means for helping to establish the date of almost any polychrome vessel from those areas.

Today, more than at almost any other pueblo, the native pottery of Santo Domingo is used for considerable service in both the everyday meals and the sacred feasts at the Kiva. On any of the many ceremonial days, one can see traditional bowls of Kiua Polychrome, well worn from years of usage, transporting delicacies to the celebrants. Usually the bowls have the owner's name or initials scratched into the surface, or painted on with fingernail polish. Water jars, usually from Acoma, are also used, still carried about on the head, supported by the concave base that is constructed for this purpose. Loaves of native bread are carried in Indian baskets on such days, the baskets usually having been obtained in trade from Indians to the west.

Today, the pottery-making industry at Santo Domingo appears to be declining. Enough is produced to keep up with their own requirements, but relatively little is sold to tourists or collectors, who prefer the more ornate, delicate, or sophisticated wares of the other more famous pottery-making villages. A few potters are now experimenting with new types of pigments and firing their pots in a commercial kiln, but only time will tell if the style can become popular with collectors.

SANTO DOMINGO: *Two water jars. Left, the designs suggest much Cochiti influence; right, these decorations are very typical of Santo Domingo, excepting the scallop pattern at the top, which is more like a Cochiti figure. Circa 1920 and 1940. Height, 30 cm. and 29 cm.* — Santa Fe Village

SANTO DOMINGO

SANTO DOMINGO: *Two very typical food bowls. Circa 1950. Diameter, 20 cm. and 24 cm.* — Santa Fe Village

SANTO DOMINGO: *A very typical water jar with red in the design. Circa 1940. Height, 24 cm.* — Ford Ruthling

SANTO DOMINGO: *Enormous Polychrome storage jar by Santana and Crucita Melcher. Circa 1965. Height, 57.5 cm.*

SANTO DOMINGO: *Two decorative vessels with red in the designs. Circa 1940. Height, 16 cm. and 15 cm.* — Santa Fe Village

Cochiti

The pottery from Cochiti Pueblo made prior to about 1800 is very similar to that of Santo Domingo. Thereafter, we speak of a Cochiti variety of Kiua Polychrome, which continues to be produced until the present time, sometimes with an appearance so close to that of the vessels from Santo Domingo that we could not be sure of a Cochiti origin except for a certain knowledge of who made the vessel.

Much more typical for Cochiti, however, is a style of pottery decoration that began to look different from standard Kiua Polychrome by 1800, and became differentiated into Cochiti Polychrome by about 1850. The earliest manifestations of a difference are seen in the relative lightness and fineness of the Cochiti design lines, and in the fussier embellishments, such as the attachment of small triangles or other simple figures to the circumferential framing lines, which virtually never are seen on the pottery of Santo Domingo Pueblo.

By 1850, other changes crept into the style of pottery, so that Cochiti Polychrome vessels look quite distinctive from those of any other type. The old design arrangement into formal panels has been replaced by a layout in which the motifs and elements are present as unrelated and isolated patterns, sometimes appearing quite disorganized. Unique for secular pottery is the appearance of symbols elsewhere reserved only for the most sacred of vessels, the zig-zag arrows representing lightning, banks of arcs depicting clouds, and the vertical lines under the clouds showing the presence of rain. Also frequently seen on Cochiti Polychrome are a variety of realistic and mythical animals, including birds, lizards, water creatures, mammals, and even humans.

When James Stevenson collected pottery from the pueblos during the earliest days of the railroad (just before 1880) he found these features on Cochiti pottery, but he was especially intrigued by the pottery sculptures at that village. He collected charming pots in the shapes of birds with spouts at their beaks and handles across their backs. A few years later he would also have found large human sculptures of the most amazing and amusing forms, some as tall as fifty centimeters or more, made by the famous potter, Seferina Sevenna. Even to the present day, it is the charming figurines of Cochiti Polychrome that have been the most popular of all their ceramics. Helen Cordero's human sculptures are now the most famous. Even with high prices, she cannot keep up with the demand. Also well known are the owls that are sculpted by several Cochiti potters.

Another type of sculpture frequently seen on Cochiti Polychrome jars and canteens is formed by attaching clay animals, especially lizards, to the otherwise usual shape of the vessel, giving the appearance of a live creature crawling up the side of the pot.

Cochiti pottery was once noted for hard firing at high temperatures. In recent years, as at many of the other villages, the wares have been fired much cooler, and the result is less strength and serviceability. Nevertheless, for charming pottery made in completely traditional ways with native materials and techniques, the wares of Cochiti Pueblo still make excellent additions to any collection.

COCHITI: *Black-on-red water jar of classic style, and a smaller revival jar by Marie C. Pacheco of Santo Domingo. Circa 1850 and 1970. Height, 23.5 cm. and 14 cm.*

COCHITI: *Two bird effigy figures of characteristic Cochiti form. Circa 1930 and 1960. Height, 15 cm. and 14 cm.* — Santa Fe Village

COCHITI: *A very fine, large dough bowl of Kiua Polychrome. Circa 1860. Height, 32 cm.* — Ford Ruthling

COCHITI: *A very large and heavy dough bowl with sacred designs. Circa 1910. Height, 27 cm.* — Santa Fe Village

COCHITI

COCHITI: *A very fine old bowl of typical form and design. Circa 1900. Height, 12.5 cm.* — Santa Fe Village

COCHITI: *Jar, possibly from Santo Domingo, with red in the designs, and a pitcher. Circa 1935. Height, 31 cm. and 21 cm.* — Santa Fe Village

COCHITI: *A storage jar with black decorations on orange-tan slip. Circa 1880. Height, 44 cm.* — Ford Ruthling

COCHITI: *Water jar showing ceremonial break in design band, and ceremonial jar. Circa 1940, 1890. Height, 24 cm. and 29.5 cm.* — Bob Ward

COCHITI: *Figurine and black-on-red bowl. Circa 1910 and 1890. Height, 29 cm.; diameter, 31 cm.*

COCHITI: *A small water jar with decoration within the mouth. Circa 1900. Height, 21 cm.* — Ford Ruthling

JEMEZ: *Pottery house with poster-paint decorations. Circa 1960. Height, 13.5 cm.*

THE PUNAME PUEBLOS

PUNAME IS AN OLD NAME referring to the pueblos to the west, meaning at this time Santa Ana and Zia. At both villages the Keres language is spoken, but in a somewhat different dialect from that used in the northeast Keres pueblos.

A third village, Jemez, also lies in the area of the Puname pueblos but its language is Towa, and its pottery traditions are quite different. Nevertheless, because of the long reliance of Jemez on Zia for decorated pottery, we include a brief discussion of that pueblo in this section.

Jemez

When the dust had settled from the great Pueblo Revolt of 1680 and the reconquest by De Vargas a dozen years later, the unhappy residents of Jemez were among the Indians who chose to leave their ancestral homes and move north to live among their former enemies, the Navajo. It was a time of tremendous sadness and upheaval, of change and adjustment, of great uncertainty for the future. Rather than surrender to the demands imposed by the Spanish conquerors, Jemez and also Zia had witnessed the destruction of their homes and the torture to the point of death of families, friends and neighbors.

In the struggle to maintain cultural continuity, much was lost. Jemez potters, in particular, never again manufactured their traditional pottery, a black-on-white style that had served them well for over four centuries.

For fifty years the pueblo refugees subsisted in exile, finally returning slowly home to their ancient villages. The Jemez people who had previously lived in several small villages, banded together at an especially fine locality, a broad valley with a permanent stream where farming was relatively easy, and gradually peace and prosperity returned.

The people from nearby Zia, in contrast, returned to their more desolate locality, atop an isolated lava-capped hill surrounded by a drier and more barren landscape. Rather than ceasing their manufacture of fine decorated pottery, the Zians continued the craft with renewed fervor, producing vessels as fine as they had ever made before.

Thus, each village had something the other needed, and something to furnish in trade. The abundant crops from Jemez left plenty for sharing with Zia, and in return Zia furnished the fine pottery needed at Jemez.

Even in recent years, some of the best examples of Zia pottery from the eighteenth century have been obtained from the old store rooms of Jemez.

For the utility pottery, especially the big cooking pots that were harder to transport, Jemez continued to rely on the products of its own craftsmen. These vessels, rough and black on the exterior but smoother inside, are quite plain in appearance, not differing very much from the utility wares made at the other nearby villages. Examples have been made until quite recently.

In addition, for the last fifty years there has been considerable experimentation with various decorated styles, few being very long-lasting or influential on the general evolution of Pueblo Indian pottery.

One of the earliest of these experiments, in the 1920s, was the production of jars shaped like those of Zia, and painted in colors of black and red. Surviving examples are rare. These vessels often have a rather unfinished look, with cursory surface polish and geometric designs that range from sloppy to fairly neat.

Subsequent short-lived experiments include a small number of guaco-painted vessels by a woman who learned the technique from a Cochiti potter, and a few Hopi-like pots by a potter who used a clay firing to an orange-yellow color.

In addition, as at Tesuque, many Jemez potters adopted the gaudy poster-paint technique for producing tourist-oriented trinkets. These are

JEMEZ: *Decorative wedding vase by Martha Toya. Circa 1975. Height, 35 cm.* — Forrest Fenn

JEMEZ: *Decorative jar by Juanita Yepa. Circa 1975. Height, 19 cm.* — Bob Ward

painted after firing with designs in an astonishing array of styles.

The most recent and prolific of the Jemez pottery styles is also the most attractive, but suffers from the use of nontraditional methods of manufacture. The vessels are in conventional form, or sculpted, notably in owl form. They are decorated with intricate patterns applied with commercial paints of traditional color after the pots have been fired. The whole surface is then sprayed with a commercial fixative, thereby preventing smearing when the pot is rubbed with a moist object, as happens to the poster-paint wares.

The designs themselves often utilize completely traditional motifs, some copied from the styles of several centuries earlier. The pigments at first glance look like the earth materials used by most of the other pueblos. Sometimes they even have the appearance of the ancient glaze-forming mineral paints.

The vessels apparently sell very well, as one can see many being offered by numerous potters at the Indian markets in Santa Fe and surrounding towns during the summer.

JEMEZ: *Left, jar by Nancy Pecos; right, jar by Luisa and Annie Panana. Circa 1962. Height, 15 cm. and 12 cm.* — Museum of New Mexico 4647/12 and 10026/12

Santa Ana

For two centuries, the residents of this small village, whose Indian name is Tamaya, have mostly lived in their farming town of Ranchitos, near the Rio Grande. Nevertheless the traditional home site is kept neat and looks ready for occupancy at a moment's notice, and on any of the special feast days it bristles with activity.

The ceramic history of Santa Ana prior to about 1750 is the same as that of Zia, insofar as we have been able to learn at this time. Thereafter, the pottery of the two pueblos is easily differentiated on the basis of one persistent difference, namely the material used to temper the clay. At Zia, crushed black basaltic rock is invariably present, giving a peppery appearance to the usually brick-red color. At Santa Ana the tradition, as at Isleta and San Felipe, is to use fine water-worn sand, with grains up to a millimeter in diameter abundantly present in the orange-tan or brick-red clay.

While some of the early Santa Ana pots closely resemble those of Zia in both form and design, others show differences in ways that soon became distinctive design features for the village. The most prominent is the presence of massive red figures in the designs, partly without black-line edging. Another is the presence of unpainted (negative) areas within the red, usually in the form of semicircles or crescents. These features were present on the pottery of Zia, Laguna, and Acoma for a brief time just before 1800, but at Santa Ana they persisted for over a century.

Prior to 1780, the jar necks on Ranchitos Polychrome, as this early Santa Ana pottery type is called, were quite short and undecorated. After 1780, with rare exceptions, the jars have taller necks with simple patterns consisting of embellished arcs. The change defines the type called Santa Ana Polychrome.

Through the nineteenth century, vessels of Santa Ana Polychrome were made for use within the village. The total production was small, so that vessels are rarely encountered today. Principal emphasis was placed on serviceability, with relatively little care being exercised in the artistic aspects. The forms are usually a bit misshapen, and the designs, while usually bold and charming, lack precision. One motif, looking like a broad, squat Eiffel Tower, appears so frequently as to be almost a Santa Ana "trademark."

As the nineteenth century progressed, the artistry progressively declined. There was little response to the commercial impetus felt at the other villages, although during the 1920s and 1930s it appears that a slight revival in the craft occurred at Santa Ana.

Thereafter, until very recently, only one potter, Dora Montoya, has been active. Her output is not prolific, but the results are visually pleasing. Carrying on nearly all of the Santa Ana ceramics traditions, she has found a ready market for everything she produces. In the last several years, Mrs. Montoya has trained some of the younger Santa Ana women to carry on the craft, which may result in a revival.

SANTA ANA: *Decorative canteen and an older water jar. Circa 1950 and 1930. Diameter, 16 cm.; height, 23 cm.*

SANTA ANA: *New and old water jars. Left, by Dora Montoya; right, Santa Ana Polychrome of earliest vintage. Circa 1960 and 1790. Height, 24 cm. and 28 cm.*

SANTA ANA: *A fine jar with "Eiffel Tower" design, showing ceremonial line breaks and red banding of the underbody. Circa 1920. Height, 28.5 cm.* — Museum of New Mexico 7783/12

SANTA ANA: *A venerable bowl that has seen much hard use. Circa 1880. Height, 12.5 cm.*

SANTA ANA: *Food bowl with very thick paint, almost a glaze, red arc designs, and single framing lines. Circa 1810. Diameter, 24.5 cm.*

SANTA ANA: *A fine old bowl of classic Santa Ana style. Circa 1810. Diameter, 22 cm.*—Museum of New Mexico 19523/12

Zia

For many centuries, Zia Pueblo has been a famous center for the manufacture of fine pottery. Prior to about 1700, they specialized in glaze-paint styles, turning thereafter exclusively to the use of a mineral matte paint.

Throughout Zia ceramics history, the one feature that can be used to identify their pottery is the invariable presence of finely crushed black basalt mixed with the clay. Modern potters from Zia complain about the back-breaking work necessary to grind the hard, dense rock, but none of them would ever think of omitting this necessary ingredient.

To collect the basalt is not a difficult chore, as it lies all about the village in abundance. Like all the other nearby flat-topped hills (called mesas), the isolated crest where Zia is perched is capped with a layer of ancient volcanic lava. A million years ago each lava bed was a depression in the broad valley of the ancient Rio Grande. With the tremendous eruptions of ash and suffocating gases emitted from the nearby Jemez Caldera, there were also flows of lava filling in the lower depressions. With the passing millenia, erosion nibbled away the material around these tough lava beds, leaving them as caps to the resulting hills.

Throughout the Historic Era, there have been no significant slumps in either quality or artistry of the Zia pottery. Perhaps this is because the poor surrounding land for agriculture forced continuous reliance on trading for food from Jemez, San Felipe, and the nearby Spanish haciendas. With fine pottery being one of their few exportable products, the Zia potters would have an unrelenting incentive to maintain the quality of their wares.

Through the eighteenth century, as at Santa Ana, the jars from Zia Pueblo are characterized by their very short undecorated necks. Bowls and jars are beautifully decorated in black and red designs on a light buckskin-tan slip, incorporating numerous versions of the ubiquitous feather symbol. Prior to about 1765, the rim tops of both bowls and jars were painted red; thereafter black was used.

Just before 1800, several changes occurred, leading to a pottery type called Trios Polychrome. Medium-size jars (water jars with concave bases) sprouted necks, which were decorated with a particular style of embellished arcs, probably derived from an ancient symbol for the cap of a feather. Enormous storage jars and bread-dough mixing bowls were constructed for the first time, these larger vessels retaining more of the eighteenth century features than the medium-size vessels. In particular, the huge storage jars have short undecorated necks, and the dough bowls carry an eighteenth-century design pattern that has persisted on such vessels almost without change until recent times.

Through the nineteenth century, the stylistic evolution of Zia pottery was slow, and the overall changes were rather mild. Jars became a little taller, with higher shoulders, but bowl forms were almost unchanged. Designs evolved from the formal layout of spirals at each end of a diagonal line and other geometric patterns, to the incorporation of elements from nature, notably birds and floral patterns. Some of the vessels of the late 1800s are especially fine, with thin walls, thick paint textures, and a nice white slip. The excellence seems not to have been a specific response to the tourist-market influence brought by the railroad, but, just as at Zuñi, simply a delightful flowering of artistry for its own sake.

Near the beginning of the present century, the mineral paint on Zia vessels changed somewhat in consistency, losing the thick blackness of previous years and becoming somewhat thinner, browner, and sometimes slightly fugitive.

In the 1920s, the potters experimented with a new type of slip. Instead of the previous white or light tan background, the color was a shade of orange, to which the black and red designs were applied. The results are very attractive, and the technique has been used occasionally, even to the present time.

There were also several changes in design style during the 1920s. Birds continue as a prominent motif, but look somewhat more relaxed and less conventionalized. A new version of the old feather symbol occurs quite frequently. Also, by 1930, the previously invariable red band below the design area was replaced by an overall red slip on the underbody of a bowl or jar.

Through the previous century, the figure of a

ZIA: *Large storage jar. Circa 1940. Height, 40 cm.*

deer or, rarely, some other mammal had sometimes been used in the designs. As the middle of the twentieth century approached, the deer figures became especially naturalistic and graceful. At the same time, another new bird style appeared, representing the roadrunner, painted in all black-colored paint with no red as in the more usual bird figures.

Commencing about 1940, the use of a slightly different clay, still always tempered with crushed basalt, resulted in a peculiar blemish that mars some of the otherwise very nice vessels of that decade. The effect was produced by small chunks of a white mineral substance that would gradually expand during the twelve or so months after firing. The force of expansion produced a flaking or scabbing of the surface, each resulting pit having a white speck at its center. Soon most potters learned to avoid the faulty clay, but some Zia pottery is still produced with this defect, which cannot be detected until several months after the vessels have been fired.

The recent Zia pottery is produced mainly for sale to tourists and collectors. Most of the vessels are still very beautiful, and attract much admiration at the annual Indian market in Santa Fe. Cooler firing to avoid blemishes means the vessels must be somewhat heavier for strength than they were a century ago. The cooler flame does not set the black mineral pigments so firmly, so that care must be exercised to avoid smearing the designs.

One fine potter, Vicentita Pino, makes a large storage jar each year, but most of the Zia craftsmen avoid this difficult task because of the tendency for such vessels to crack during the firing. Until about 1955, there were several other excellent potters who also made very large vessels. Now the principal output is in the form of small jars, five to thirty centimeters in height.

At least one recent artist has been painting very naturalistic designs of human dancers on Zia pots, using a variety of new pigments encompassing a full range of colors.

ZIA: *Storage jar with orange slip characteristic of the 1920s. Circa 1920. Height, 29 cm.* — Museum of New Mexico 11135/12

ZIA: *A fine and exuberant jar with designs borrowed from Zuñi Pueblo. Circa 1890. Height, 24 cm.*

ZIA: *The classic dough bowl, in this case with especially graceful form. Circa 1850. Height, 26 cm.* — Forrest Fenn

ZIA: *A fine jar by the prize-winning potter, Vicentita Pino. Circa 1960. Height, 24 cm.*

ZIA: *A beautiful and well-used water jar with classical nineteenth-century designs. Circa 1890. Height, 32.5 cm.* — Ford Ruthling

ZIA: *Water jar and bowl. Circa 1900. Height, 23 cm.; diameter, 29 cm.* — Santa Fe Village

ZIA: *Recent version of the classic dough bowl. Circa 1950. Height, 27 cm.* — Ford Ruthling

ACOMA: *Left, a wedding vase by Lucy M. Lewis; middle, an eye-dazzler jar by Lucy M. Lewis; right, an older wedding vase. Made in 1962, 1959 and circa 1920. Height, 23 cm., 10.5 cm., 41 cm.*

THE WESTERN KERES PUEBLOS

Acoma

Acoma, the Sky City, has been located atop its isolated mesa in west-central New Mexico for nearly seven centuries. With occasional exceptions, every period of Acoma ceramics has shone with excellence.

During the prehistoric glaze-ware days, Acoma was one of the rare producers of stunning dark, olive-green glaze. On a milky white background of well-fired pottery, the results were spectacular. Unfortunately, no complete vessels are known to have survived. Through the sixteenth and seventeenth centuries, the background color became a shade of warm buckskin-tan; the decorations, only rarely green at this stage, were exuberant in their use of rich, shiny glaze and matte-red colors. Especially in the seventeenth century, as the manufacture of glaze ware drew to an end, the ceramics of Acoma reached one of the technical and artistic heights rarely surpassed by any Stone Age people in the world. The pottery type, called Hawikuh Polychrome, is named for a Zuñi-area village further west, but the product at Acoma, which will someday receive its own distinctive type name, was consistently better than the vessels from Hawikuh. Today, the rare vessels that survive are cherished treasures in a few museums.

At about 1700, three changes occurred in the pottery styles of Acoma. The glaze paint was replaced by a mineral matte pigment. The basal area of the jars was changed from the previously convex form to concave, which afforded greater stability on a flat surface, and facilitated carrying the vessels on a person's head. The third change was to a somewhat taller, narrower jar form, the underbody gently flaring from the base, surmounted by a bulging upper body, the whole resembling a large mushroom.

This style of pottery, called Ako Polychrome, had no neck on the jars, only a tiny flare to form a slight lip. By 1760, however, the potters began to see the advantage of a neck, and commenced to fashion a vertical, cylindrical structure for this purpose, resulting in a new type we call Acomita Polychrome.

At first the vessels of Acomita Polychrome were much like their ancestor, but soon the presence of a neck on the jars was joined by other traits that enable us also to distinguish bowls of the type from those made earlier. The pots are much heavier, often somewhat misshapen in form, and the designs are much less formal in their arrangement. By 1800, the vessels took on a close resemblance to those of Santa Ana, but this phase was only a brief one at Acoma.

Through the nineteenth century, Acoma pottery, perhaps influenced by the trends at Zia, evolved in both form and design into the styles of Acoma Polychrome that are so familiar even today. Designs became more floral, and birds, especially parrots, were painted in a variety of beautiful patterns. The transitional pottery type during the middle 1800s is known as McCartys Polychrome.

When James Stevenson came to collect artifacts for the United States National Museum on the earliest of the railroad excursions, he found McCartys Polychrome vessels that look very much like some of the Acoma Polychrome pots produced there at present. What he did not see, however, was the profusion of additional styles that were to be made at that village in the succeeding years. By 1900, one course of the development resulted in a decorative style with a profusion of interconnected geometric figures, including zigzags, hatchured areas, spirals, stairsteps, and similar figures filling virtually all the available area of the vessel. As the twentieth century progressed, another "eye-dazzler" style was invented which surpasses all other pueblo pottery design in the complex precision of its line work. The patterns covering all the available area are formed of intersecting or angling parallel lines, very close together and very evenly spaced. Enormous concentration, patience and muscular control are required to execute these designs.

A third line of development turned to the inspiration of prehistoric pottery design, especially of the famous Mimbres culture in southwestern New Mexico at around 1100 A.D. The motifs include a fascinating zoo of real and imaginary animals, birds, and bugs. These the Acoma artists copied with much precision in designs of black lines only.

In many cases the innovative designs have

ACOMA: *Two fine water jars. Circa 1940. Height, 20 cm. and 32 cm.*

been painted on a host of new vessel forms, ranging from squat jars closing in on themselves to leave only a tiny opening, to graceful vases that are very tall and slender. Pottery was also sculpted in bird forms, such as owls and turkeys.

Even to the present day, much pottery is made at Acoma, continuing the tradition for thin, hard pottery, beautifully decorated, that has distinguished the ceramics of this village for centuries. Only one defect has arisen to mar the excellence of the Acoma wares. For the past several decades, some of the pots, as at Zia, have suffered from the presence of a material in the clay that swells during the first year or so after the pot is fired, flaking off bits of the surface.

ACOMA: *Canteen of McCartys Polychrome. Circa 1880. Height, 20 cm.*

ACOMA: *Water jar with no red in the designs; white jar showing a coiled-and-punched technique made by Stella Shutiva. Circa 1930, 1970. Height, 18 cm.* — Bob Ward

ACOMA

ACOMA: *A fine water jar with designs from Zuñi Pueblo. Circa 1900. Height, 29 cm.*

ACOMA: *Well-used food bowl with red-painted, sculptured rim. Circa 1940. Diameter, 23 cm.*

COCHITI AND ACOMA: *Two owl figurines, the left one from Cochiti by Seferina Ortiz; the right one from Acoma by W. Aragon. Circa 1950. Height, 20 cm.*

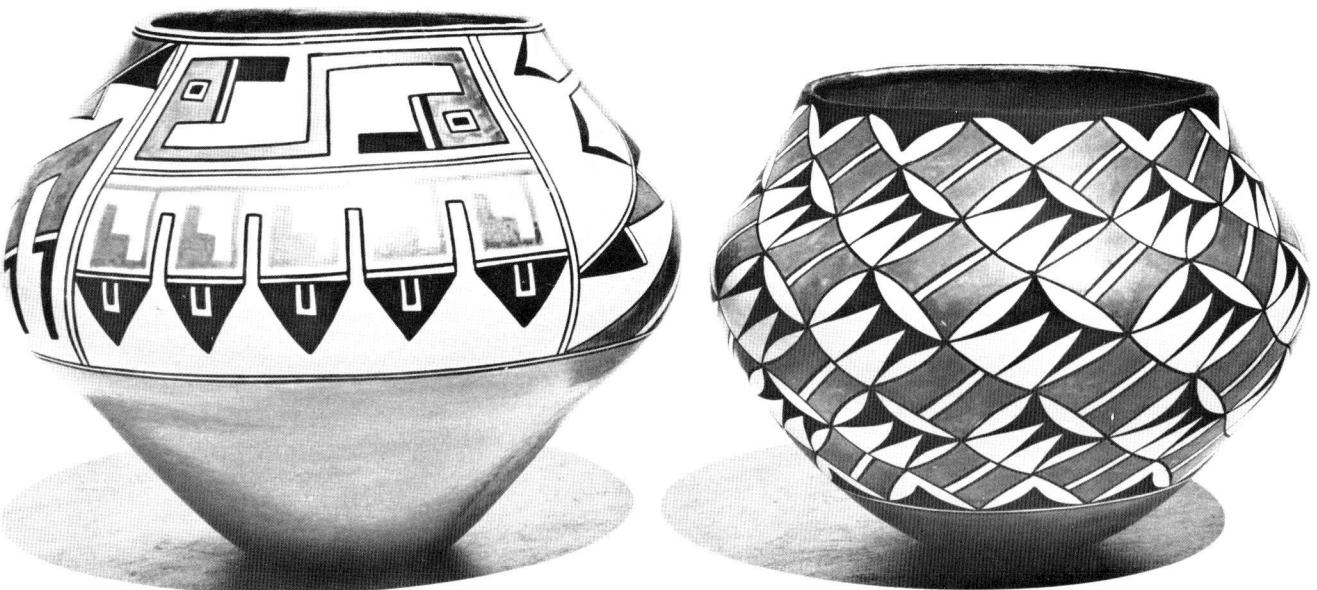

ACOMA: *Two superb jars by Anita Lowden, the left one in the style of ancient Ako Polychrome. Circa 1965. Height, 18 cm. and 16 cm.*

ACOMA: *Jar of especially unusual form, but with a design style at least nine centuries old. Circa 1930. Height, 26 cm.*—John Rivenburgh

ACOMA

ACOMA: *Two unusual jars. Left, orange-red color with no painted design; right, white-on-red with stamped arrow pattern around the top. Circa 1960. Height, 16.5 cm. and 12.5 cm.* — Bob Ward

ACOMA: *Seed-jar bowl shape with polychrome designs. Circa 1940. Height, 17.5 cm.* — Ford Ruthling

ACOMA: *Jar with heart-line-deer decorations by the famous potter, Lucy M. Lewis. Circa 1960. Height, 12 cm.* — Ford Ruthling

Laguna

The pueblo of Laguna was established relatively recently. After the Indian revolt of 1680 and the subsequent reconquest, many of the Pueblo Indians were uprooted from their ancestral homes. Some moved to the area of their former enemies, the Navajo, and remained there for up to fifty years. Others banded together to form new villages, of which Laguna Pueblo is one. At first the pottery of Laguna was almost indistinguishable from that of Acoma. Even through the early years of this century the ceramics styles of the two villages have continued to be very similar. But, while Acoma has maintained a prodigious output until the present time, the manufacture of pottery at Laguna Pueblo came nearly to an end in the early 1900s, with only a very small number of vessels being produced there in recent years.

Accordingly, surviving vessels from Laguna are relatively rare, and the finest examples command very high prices. Because of their similarity to vessels from Acoma, it is important to have the origin of any questionable vessel authenticated by an expert.

As a rule, the vessels from Laguna Pueblo are distinguished from those of Acoma by one or more of the following traits:

1. The slip is polished by stone, with the stroke marks showing. (Acoma pots usually do not show such polishing marks.)

2. The vessel is relatively heavy and thick-walled for its size.

3. The clay has a greater abundance of sand and dark fragments of amorphous or stony material for temper. (The *predominant* tempering

LAGUNA: *Two beautiful parrot jars. The smaller has thick dense paint, especially characteristic of some late pottery from Laguna. Circa 1910. Height, 30 cm. and 20 cm.* — Santa Fe Village

material at both Acoma and Laguna is crushed pieces of old pottery.)

4. The interior of a bowl is more likely to be red slipped, and the interior of a jar may have some red slip coarsely brushed across the surface.

5. The underbody of a jar is more likely to be slightly concave in vertical profile, especially just below the design area. (The *base* of the jar at either Acoma or Laguna is almost always concave for carrying on the head.)

6. The designs are usually less precise in execution, and often are composed of black-edged red areas connected together at their tips in such a way that the red itself joins together between adjacent designs. (This latter design feature also occurs somewhat at Acoma and Zia, and is especially characteristic of the pottery period 1880–1900.)

In about 1880 some of the Laguna Indians moved to the Rio Grande pueblo of Isleta, establishing a suburb called Oraibi (not the Hopi village in Arizona of the same name), where they made a style of pottery that is distinctly different from either the classic Isleta style (a river-sand-tempered plain redware) or the parent Laguna style. Sometimes called Isleta Polychrome, the usually small tourist-market vessels are made with a tan, finely sandy clay and slipped with a milk-white material of very distinctive appearance. The designs are nicely executed in brownish-black mineral paint and red clay. Little bowls with handles are relatively common. At present these pieces are rare, and considered to be desirable antiques.

The Isleta variety of Laguna pottery has recently evolved into a type that is made of commercial clay and constructed by non-traditional techniques, and accordingly lies outside the scope of a discussion of Indian wares.

LAGUNA: *Two superb vessels. The thick, black paint on the handled jar has partially vitrified to a glaze. Circa 1880 and 1900. Height, 25.5 cm. and 23.5 cm.* — Santa Fe Village

ISLETA: *Three little bowls with Laguna-influenced designs. Circa 1900. Diameter, 11 cm.; 10 cm.; 14 cm.* — Santa Fe Village

LAGUNA: *Decorative jar with both red and orange in the designs. Circa 1900. Height, 31.5 cm.* — Ford Ruthling

LAGUNA: *Polychrome bowl with red interior. Circa 1920. Diameter, 26.5 cm.*

ZUNI: *A superb example of classic Zuñi pottery. Circa 1880. Height, 23 cm.* — Museum of New Mexico 18767/12

THE ASHIWI PUEBLOS

FED BY RUMORS of fabulous treasure, the sixteenth-century Spanish conquerors of Montezuma pushed ever farther in their quests for gold and silver. In Peru the discoveries exceeded even the wildest dreams, enhancing ever more the credibility of any other tales of riches that reached Mexico City. No wonder, then, that expeditions of hardy warriors pushed north to seek the fabled Seven Cities of Cibola, where even the dishes were said to be made of gold.

The first of these scouting trips to reach the Pueblo Indians was led by Coronado through the years surrounding 1540, and the first of the villages they encountered was Hawikuh, an Ashiwi Pueblo near the present village of Zuñi.

Coronado dispatched his emissaries in all directions to look for precious metals and other evidence of treasure, but they found none. Instead of golden dishes, they found utensils of clay. The only treasure was the rich harvest of souls to be saved, and the Franciscan Fathers accompanying the expedition wasted little time in planning their mission.

Nearly sixty more years of sporadic exploration were to pass, however, before the Padres got their chance, but the first permanent settlement was far from the Ashiwi area and accordingly had relatively little effect on these and the even further Hopi Pueblos.

Prior to about 1700, the Ashiwi ceramic history resembled that of Acoma in the production of a similar sequence of glaze-decorated vessels as well as some matte-paint vessels like those made by the Hopi Indians. At about 1700 the Ashiwi villages all consolidated at a new site called Zuñi, the smaller surrounding villages being only partially occupied thereafter, mainly as farming headquarters. Just as at Acoma, this date is also associated with the abandonment of glaze-decorated pottery and the adoption of concave bases for the jars.

The new style, called Ashiwi Polychrome, is somewhat more distinctive from the contemporary Acoma pottery than during the previous century. Paradoxically, the Zuñi pottery more closely resembles the wares from much more distant Zia, in both the shapes of the jars and the designs used to decorate their surfaces.

The contrasts with Zia wares, however, are certainly distinct enough for the use of different type names. The basic distinction is in the materials of manufacture. At Zia the basalt-tempered clay fires to a peppery brick-red color. At Zuñi the clay fires to a white color with gray core, and is coarsely tempered with crushed fragments of older pots.

Another distinction is in the decoration below the design area. Puname Polychrome jars from

ZUNI: *A view of the pueblo as photographed by Ben Wittick, circa 1890.* — Museum of New Mexico, Photo Archives

Zia usually have an encircling row of red arcs, and the underbody is red banded. Ashiwi Polychrome never has the arcs, and the underbody is all red in color.

The trend to more utilitarian forms throughout the Pueblo world in about 1760 led to Kiapkwa Polychrome at Zuñi, where, however, there were more residual traces of sculpture than at most of the other pueblos. Because the base of a jar was usually molded in a cup-shaped vessel, the clay bulged out at the top of this underbody part, and the bulge was not smoothed away. Also, there usually is a fairly sharp angle where the incurving body of the jar meets the more vertical neck. This last is also usually sculptured at the top with a slightly out-flaring lip.

Until about 1760, the rim tops of jars and bowls made at Zuñi were painted red; thereafter the color was black. The completely red underbody persisted a little longer, until 1800, and thereafter, in a style unique to the Pueblo world, the underbody was almost invariably colored black or very dark brown.

In the middle of the nineteenth century, Zuñi Polychrome evolved, being distinguished almost entirely on the basis of design. Jar forms show a slight change, usually towards moving the position of greatest width to a greater height above the base, creating, as at Acoma and Zia, a shouldered look.

In 1879, James Stevenson was especially attracted to the pottery of Zuñi, as well he might, for then the vessels of that village were both well constructed and artistically decorated. His collections for the United States National Museum in Washington included some magnificent examples, and many others from the prolific Zuñi output of that period are preserved as prize specimens in both private and public collections.

The excellence persisted until shortly after 1900 and then began to decline. Vessel walls became thicker, and cooler firing robbed them of their previous strength. Artistry persisted for a while, although the sculptural features (the slight underbody bulge and the tiny lip) were usually omitted. By 1940, the output was very little, artistry generally suffered and the Zuñi ceramics history virtually terminated. In the subsequent years, only a few vessels have been made.

One feature of Zuñi pottery that differs from that of other villages is the large number of sacred terraced bowls that were manufactured. These prayer-meal bowls have stair-step sculptures on their rims, sometimes a handle across the opening, and are decorated in a very characteristic style, employing representations of frogs, tadpoles, dragonflies and mythical serpents with red lines from mouth to heart. All of these are associated with water, which the Pueblo Indians are always in danger of lacking, and must seek through prayerful ceremonies.

During the late nineteenth century, when Zuñi pottery making was going through one of its finest periods, the design elements that were used are surprisingly few in number. Among the most notable is the peculiarly Zuñi deer, with "heart line," a red line from mouth to chest and an arrowhead at the heart position. The same motif has been used on Polacca Polychrome, made by the Hopi Indians, and more recently at Acoma. At Zuñi, the deer always stands in a house composed of two feathers that join above the animal figure.

Decoration on the body of a Zuñi jar is usually arranged in four panels, alternating wide and narrow. The wide panels are usually the more innovative, containing such designs as the heart-line deer, a line of little red birds, a huge sunflower pattern, and almost invariably a variety of spiral elements or stairstep figures with cross-hatched filling. The necks of jars are usually decorated with more geometric figures, but rarely birds have been used.

Bowls are decorated on the interior with figures much like those in the larger panels on the body of a jar. The inside of the rim area is usually an encircling band of some simple figure. The exteriors of bowls are almost invariably the same, with diagonal lines, each embellished by a pair of stylized feather symbols. The conservative persistence of this one decoration style for bowl exteriors is like the same persistence of a somewhat different pattern on the exterior of dough bowls at Zia from 1800 to the present.

As at so many of the other pottery-making pueblos, Zuñi potters have long persisted in put-

ZUNI: *A crude but powerful ceremonial jar with frogs, butterflies and dragonflies. Circa 1890. Height, 21 cm.*

ting a "ceremonial break" into every line that would otherwise encircle a pot. This feature, with nearly a thousand-year history of usage on pueblo pottery, consists of a short gap in the otherwise complete line. The original meaning is lost in antiquity, but modern potters allude to such ideas as a path for the pot's spirit to enter and leave, or a safeguard against trapping the potter's spirit into the vessel. At some villages, like Tesuque, the line break has been conscientiously omitted for several centuries. At others, like Acoma and Zia, it is usually present but generally very inconspicuous. Santo Domingo and Cochiti almost invariably put in the break, sometimes with such prominence that it constitutes part of the design. Zuñi is almost in this last category, especially for the heavy lines around the shoulder of a jar or around the interior of a bowl, below the rim design.

ZUNI: *Bird effigy. Circa 1890. Height, 14 cm.* — Santa Fe Village

ZUNI: *Classic style of water jar, showing the effects of much service. Circa 1890. Height, 25 cm.* — Ford Ruthling

ZUNI: *Three fine jars with classic form and design. Circa 1890. Height, 12.5 cm., 12.5 cm., 20.5 cm.* — Santa Fe Village

ZUNI: *Owl effigy and bowl in the form of a ceremonial vessel, replete with sacred designs. Circa 1950. Height, 22.5 cm.; diameter, 25 cm.*

ZUNI: *Bowl with heart-line-deer figures. Circa 1905. Diameter, 37 cm.*

ZUNI: *Sacred prayer-meal bowl with frog and tadpole design. Circa 1890. Maximum diameter, 26 cm.* — Bob Ward

HOPI: *Two jars of Hano Polychrome with coiled-and-corrugated sculpture on the neck, the right one by Nampeyo. Circa 1920. Height, 16 cm. and 29 cm.* — Forrest Fenn

THE HOPI PUEBLOS

LEGENDS OF GOLDEN DISHES in the fabled Seven Cities of Cibola very likely arose from the orange or yellow pottery made by the Hopi Indians in what is now northeastern Arizona. Coronado and the other sixteenth-century treasure-hungry explorers could tell the difference at a glance, but to the Indians who knew almost nothing about metal, the distinction was less clear. Questioned with a sample of true gold to examine, the Indians likely intended no deception as they pointed northwards and told of dishes made with the same material.

Clay that fires to shades of yellow and orange has been the standard Hopi ceramic material for six centuries. This clay is perhaps the finest of any that is available in the southwest. Carefully fired, it hardens to a very dense, tough pottery, whose broken pieces clink when hit together, rather than thud like the Tewa pottery.

Five hundred years ago, the Hopis were using this clay to form an especially fine and artistic pottery type called Sikyatki Polychrome, named for a village that was abandoned before the Europeans arrived. When J. W. Fewkes excavated the ruins of Sikyatki in the 1890s, both he and the Hopi workmen marveled at the magnificent ancient pottery they uncovered. Indeed the wife of one of the workmen, a woman from the Tewa-speaking Hano Pueblo named Nampeyo, was so inspired by the fragments of pottery she saw from Sikyatki that she resolved to duplicate both the excellence and the style of the ancient ware.

In the years between Sikyatki Polychrome and Nampeyo's revival, the pottery of the Hopi area had gone through several major changes. The first was a gradual decadence of Sikyatki Polychrome itself, leading to an intermediate pottery type called San Bernardo Polychrome, which is thick, heavy, carelessly formed, and decorated with indifference.

In about 1700, immigrants from the Rio Grande area, seeking to escape from the turmoil of revolt and reconquest, settled in several new Hopi area villages, notably Payupki and Hano. With the influx of people came new pottery ideas, from which Payupki Polychrome evolved. The village of Payupki did not survive for long, but Hano, built on First Mesa near Walpi Pueblo, is still active. In contrast to the language at Walpi and the other Hopi Pueblos, the inhabitants at Hano still speak the Tewa language of their Rio Grande ancestors. Today, with Sichomovi village squeezed between Walpi and Hano, there is nearly a continuous occupation across the top of the mesa.

Payupki Polychrome vessels are very rare today. The few remaining examples show abundant feather symbols like those in vogue during the first half of the eighteenth century.

Prior to the influence from the eastern pueblos, Hopi pottery was generally unslipped, with painted decorations being applied to the well-polished clay body itself. Sometime during the eighteenth century, however, Hopi potters began to experiment with the use of a slip, which usually contracted at a different rate during firing so that the surface is minutely crazed or crackled. The predominant Hopi pottery type with this feature is called Polacca Polychrome, which was made until about 1900. Also produced during the same period was an unslipped type called Walpi Polychrome, whose manufacture continues to the present.

Nampeyo probably made both types at the time of Fewkes's excavations at Sikyatki. She and her neighbors on First Mesa had responded to the influence of the railroad, producing attractive vessels for tourists and collectors, and at the same time making jars and bowls for their own domestic use.

Nampeyo's revival of the ancient Sikyatki styles, however, so eclipsed the currently produced pottery in both excellence of construction and artistry that the manufacture of Walpi Polychrome was much curtailed, and Polacca Polychrome was altogether abandoned. Her new pottery type is sufficiently distinctive that we refer to it by a separate type name, Hano Polychrome.

The most distinctive differences between Hano Polychrome and Walpi Polychrome are in the designs. Both types are unslipped, with red and black designs over an orange-yellow, sometimes mottled, background. Hano Polychrome designs utilize spiral bird beaks, feathers, and a host of

HOPI: *Typical jar and "mutton-stew" bowl of Polacca Polychrome. Circa 1880. Height, 16.5 and 16 cm.*

figures adapted from the ancient Sikyatki pottery. Walpi Polychrome designs are usually more angular and geometric, or else have the naturalistic bird and floral patterns or Zuñi-like motifs of the nineteenth century. Vessel forms also differ between the two types, those of Walpi Polychrome usually being somewhat more utilitarian, with flared rim mutton-stew bowls, and relatively globular jars.

Both types suffer from several defects not seen on the ancient Sikyatki Polychrome. The modern paint is somewhat softer and more easily smeared by rubbing. Also the modern types have somewhat heavier, softer walls. In appearance, however, they can be very beautiful indeed, especially when crafted by the half dozen or so of the most talented artisans.

For many years the only appreciable production of Hopi Indian pottery has been confined to the three villages on First Mesa. Since the time of Nampeyo, both quantity and quality have remained remarkably high, although, as at any of the pueblos, there are some potters who make poor examples.

Through this period there has been little change in style, the principal innovation being the experimentation with slip. Two new types have been developed, one with a pure white slip, decorated in black and red, and the other with red slip, decorated with black and white.

Anyone displaying the finest Hopi pottery of recent years can take much pleasure from both the beauty of the vessel and from the centuries of tradition that lie behind its manufacture.

HOPI: *Left, Sichomovi Polychrome jar with birds by Nampeyo; center, Polacca Polychrome double-spouted jar; right, Hano Polychrome jar. Circa 1920, 1880, 1940. Diameter, 27 cm., 16 cm., 30 cm.*

HOPI: *Shallow bowl, drilled before firing for hanging on the wall. The kachina face has been popular since about 1880. Circa 1950. Diameter, 22 cm.*

HOPI: *Wedding vase with pure white slip by Fawn. Circa 1970. Height, 29 cm.* — Forrest Fenn

HOPI: *A finely painted polychrome jar with pure white slip. Circa 1960. Height, 23 cm.*

HOPI

HOPI: *Polacca Polychrome effigy jar, probably made for ceremonial purposes. Circa 1880. Width, 17.5 cm.* — Forrest Fenn

HOPI: *Three vases of Hano Polychrome. Circa 1920. Height (tallest), 25.5 cm.* — Santa Fe Village

MARICOPA: *Two jars and a bowl of very typical style. Circa 1950. Height, 42 cm., 13 cm., 42 cm.*

THE OTHER SOUTHWESTERN INDIANS

IT IS THE PUEBLO INDIANS who are the masters of pottery making, but several other tribes in the area make noteworthy ceramic vessels, which are discussed briefly here.

Maricopa

In south-central Arizona, the Maricopa Indians have long fashioned a very distinctive style of pottery with black designs on a red or white background. The red pots are especially characteristic, the slip being a particular shade of cherry red, highly polished. The white is actually a light brownish-grey color. The pots are fired before being decorated, the designs then applied with thick mesquite juice, which is baked on at a low temperature near the fire.

MARICOPA: *This bowl has the usual well-polished red interior, and a black-on-white exterior design. Circa 1950. Diameter, 17 cm.*

Mojave

Somewhat resembling the ancient Hohokam pottery of southern Arizona, Mojave ceramics are decorated with red mineral paint on an unslipped tan background. The designs are principally geometric in a rather distinctive style of angular lines with triangular fillings at each corner. Some effigy figures have been made in recent years, but the production has now virtually ceased.

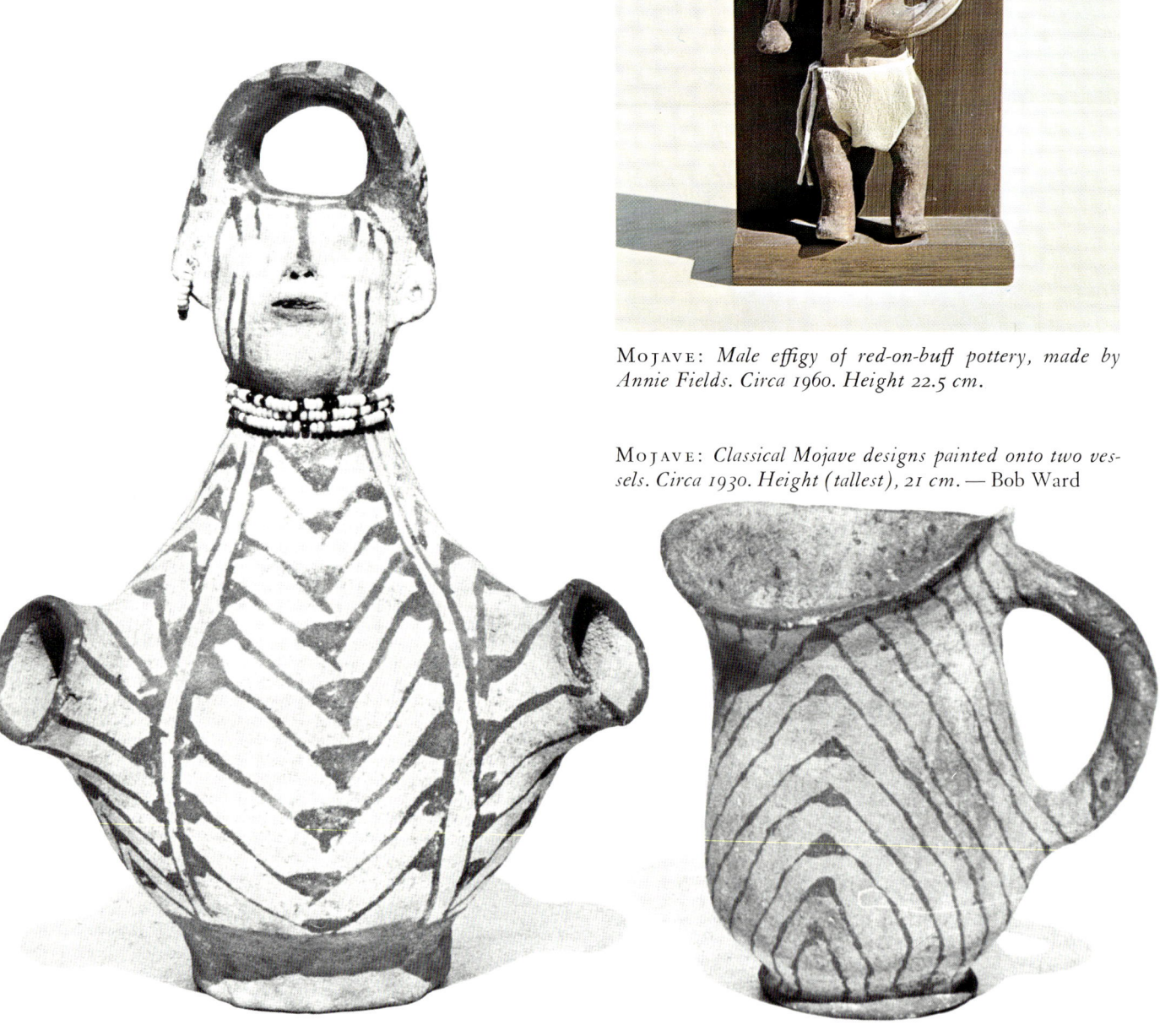

MOJAVE: *Male effigy of red-on-buff pottery, made by Annie Fields. Circa 1960. Height 22.5 cm.*

MOJAVE: *Classical Mojave designs painted onto two vessels. Circa 1930. Height (tallest), 21 cm.* — Bob Ward

MOJAVE / PAPAGO

MOJAVE: *Three figurines. The frog legend says that when the people were on an island, freezing with cold, no one could get fire to the people until the frog brought a burning stick. The woman effigy has beaded necklace and earrings, and real human hair on her head. The multi-spouted effigy is similarly beaded. Circa 1950. Height of the woman (center), 16 cm.*

Papago

The Papago potters are especially noted for their large jars, some being among the largest pottery vessels made by the Southwest Indians. Like the other southern Arizona desert tribes, the Papagos use the ancient paddle-and-anvil method for thinning and shaping the walls of their vessels. A rock is held on the interior as an anvil, while the exterior is pounded with a simple paddle. Like the Mojaves, the Papagos decorate their unslipped brown pots with a mineral pigment that fires red in the oxidizing flame. Designs often include rather coarse spirals. Many of the large Papago jars, however, are completely undecorated.

PAPAGO: *A very typical jar with rust-red designs on brownish-tan clay. Circa 1900. Height, 42 cm.*

Navajo

When Pueblo refugees settled with the Navajos in about 1700, a new pottery type emerged, called Gobernador Polychrome. From this descended a series of decorated Navajo styles. At first the pottery was relatively fine, but gradually the clay became coarser, the construction heavier and sloppier, and the firing uneven. Design influence from all pueblo areas is present in the earlier types, with Cochiti and other Rio Grande pueblo influence apparently predominant during the nineteenth century. The designs are usually painted in brownish-red mineral paint.

The Navajos are better known for their utility pottery, which has no painted designs. Usually in jar form, the pots have rounded or pointed bottoms or else a very small flattening for precarious support. There is often some crude sculpturing in the form of ribbons or fillets of clay around the top, with nicks for decoration. The color is usually a dark brown, or black if well used in the cooking fire. New pots are often sealed with pitch to make them waterproof.

NAVAJO: *A typical Navajo decorated jar; and a small vessel, possibly ceremonial, utilizing Hopi clay for the body. Circa 1870. Height, 25 cm. and 11.5 cm.*

NAVAJO: *Red-on-buff double-handled jar and pitch-covered utility jar with zig-zag sculpture below the rim. Circa 1940. Height, 17 cm. and 21 cm.* — Museum of New Mexico 8027/12 and 3578/12

YUMA: *A heavy little pitcher made before the Nazi Germany swastika became unpopular. Circa 1910. Height, 13 cm.* — Santa Fe Village

Chihuahua

Part of the ancient Southwest Indian domain extends into the northern part of Chihuahua, Mexico, where Casas Grandes and related ruins have yielded superb pottery of the twelfth through fourteenth centuries. In recent years, the popularity of these ceramics pieces, especially the effigy vessels, has resulted in a revival of the styles that were made much earlier. Much of this revival ware is relatively crude, and unfortunately, most of it is artificially weathered and aged and sold as genuine prehistoric artifacts. Recently, however, in the town of Mata Ortiz, Juan Quezada has been sparking a revival of pottery making inspired by the ancient Casas Grandes wares, but with no attempt at misrepresentation. Indeed, the finest of Quezada's pots are signed on the bottom by the artist before firing, in order to avoid completely the accusation of creating fakes. The manufacture of these fine wares has been observed in detail by Spencer MacCallum, who describes a technique that follows completely the traditions of construction by hand with native materials and firing in the ancient way without a kiln. The results are well-made, hard-fired, and beautiful, as Quezada is both a superb craftsman and a precise draftsman of attractive designs.

CHIHUAHUA: *Two fine jars by Juan Quezada in ancient Casas Grandes style. Circa 1976. Height, 19 cm.*

GLOSSARY

BAND. A design region extending around a pot, bounded above and below by framing lines.

BASE. The supporting area of a vessel, at the very bottom.

BLACK-ON-BLACK. A decorative technique in which the designs are delineated by means of dull black paint on a shiny black background, invented at San Ildefonso just prior to 1920 and used there and at Santa Clara until the present.

CARBON PAINT. A black-firing pigment made by boiling the tender, young leaves and stems of certain plants to a thick brown juice. The material soaks into the surface and chars to a black color when the pot is fired. When made from the Rocky Mountain bee plant, the carbon paint is called guaco.

CEREMONIAL BREAK. A short gap in any design line painted completely around the vessel. Originating a thousand years ago, the original significance is lost in antiquity. The line break is sometimes called a "spirit path."

CEREMONIAL VESSEL. A pot with special designs and/or form denoting association with the native religious ceremonies that are still of great importance to the Indians. Stair-step sculpture of the rim is common on both bowls and jars of this kind, and the special designs often include the symbols for clouds, rain, lightning and feathers, as well as realistic depictions of plumed serpents, frogs, dragonflies and other water creatures.

CLAY. A mineral substance of very fine texture which, when wet, can be molded into vessels or other shapes and when fired becomes hard and relatively immune to softening again with water. Clay may be used for the body of a vessel, for covering the surface (see slip) or as paint for decorating the surface.

COCHITI SLIP. Also called Domingo slip, this material is a fine clay that can be polished by rubbing with fabric or soft leather. Used at Santo Domingo and Cochiti for centuries, the slip has also been exported to the nearby Tewa Pueblos since about 1907.

CRAZING. The very fine cracks that appear on the surface of a vessel after firing, as a result of different expansion and contraction rates for the clay in the body of the pot and the slip.

DESIGN. An overall plan of decoration, employing various motifs, each being made of one or more elements.

ELEMENTS. The simplest parts of a design or motif, from which the whole pattern is to be constructed.

FAKE. A pot constructed or altered in such a way as to intentionally deceive the viewer into

GLOSSARY

thinking it is different from what it actually is. Unfortunately, there are numerous fakes circulating through the Southwest. Common examples have been made to look like Zuñi ceremonial jars with attached bone fetishes, Casas Grandes pots of the fourteenth century, Mimbres bowls with human or animal pictures, Santa Clara black storage jars, and various Pre-Colombian figurines from Mexico. New styles of fakes are appearing regularly and the collector must be continuously wary. The best protection against purchasing a fake is to have the piece examined by an expert.

FIRE CLOUD. A darkened area on the surface of a vessel, caused by the incomplete burning of a piece of fuel that has fallen against the pot during the firing.

FIRING. A heating process by which the pottery vessel is hardened. The traditional technique does not use a kiln, the fuel simply being piled around the pots and set on fire. A reducing fire excludes fresh air from the center, resulting in pottery that may be black or a gray tone of white. An oxidizing fire allows for a draft of fresh air to permeate to the center, burning the fuel brightly and cleanly, resulting in a red surface or a creamy white, tan, yellow or orange color.

FRAMING LINE. Any circumferential line adjacent to a design area. They often occur in pairs, and sometimes are broken with a short ceremonial gap.

FUEL. The substance burned during firing. Examples are dried cow dung, slabs of bark, sticks, and coal.

GLAZE. A finely powdered mineral substance painted on the surface of a vessel which melts during firing and forms a more-or-less glassy coating. The Pueblo Indians used this material only for painting the design lines, not for overall waterproofing, until as late as about 1700. Thereafter the use of glaze paint was abandoned in favor of carbon or matte-mineral paints.

GUACO. The name given to cakes of dried plant juice that can be dissolved for use as carbon paint.

KILN. An enclosure for firing pottery, not used by the Pueblo Indians except insofar as a kiln is formed by the fuel itself piled over the vessels.

LINE BREAK. *See* CEREMONIAL BREAK.

LIP. A tiny flare at the opening of a vessel to reduce dribble during the pouring of a liquid.

MATTE PAINT. A substance used for decorating pottery which does not melt during the firing; the opposite of glaze paint.

MINERAL PAINT. A substance used for decorating pottery formed of a finely powdered mineral substance such as iron oxide, mixed with water, and perhaps even including some carbonaceous material as a binder.

MOTIF. A recognizable part of an overall design, composed of one or several elements.

NECK. Part of a jar near the opening which is relatively constricted and cylindrical in comparison with the main body of the vessel. Some jars have no neck.

PANEL. A rectangular section of a design band.

PASTE. The fired mixture of clay and temper that forms the structure of the pot.

POLISH. The smooth surface finish achieved by means of stone stroking or rubbing with fabric or leather when the surface is still damp before firing.

POLYCHROME. A decorative style in which three or more colors (usually black, red and white) enter into the overall decorations of the vessel. The designation often enters into pottery type names, for example Tesuque Polychrome, abbreviated Tesuque P.

RIM. The region of the vessel adjacent to the opening.

GLOSSARY

SHERD. A piece of broken pottery.

SHOULDER. The widest part of a jar, if it occurs rather high on the vessel.

SLIP. An especially fine clay, mopped in a watery suspension onto the surface of the vessel. The color is usually a shade of white or red.

TEMPER. An inert substance mixed with the clay to reduce stickiness, decrease cracking when the newly formed pot is dried, and help the pot to fire better. Typical tempering materials are fine sand, powdered rock, and pulverized sherds.

TOURIST. A visitor to the Southwest. Here the connotation refers to a person with at least passing interest in the cultural attractions of the area. His taste may range from completely inexperienced in Indian arts and crafts to thoroughly sophisticated. He is the inspiration for both "tourist junk" at the one extreme and for some of the finest and most exciting revivals in artistry and craftsmanship at the other. The tourist market has furnished the basic financial support for the production of Indian pottery since 1880, helping to perpetuate an ancient craft that would have otherwise become nearly extinct. Museums and "serious collectors" accordingly owe the visitors to this area a much greater debt than is implied by the disparaging connotation that often is now associated with the word "tourist."

TYPE. The designation given to a group of pots all quite similar to each other. The group is given a type name, for example, Santa Clara Black.

UNDERBODY. The lower parts of a vessel, below the design area, or below the widest part if undecorated, or below a low bend or groove in the surface if such is present.

UPPERBODY. The parts of the vessel above the middle body if such is clearly delineated by bends in the surface or by design layout, or, if there is no such delineation, the parts of the vessel above the underbody.

VEGETAL PAINT. *See* CARBON PAINT.

SELECTED READING

The Pottery of Santo Domingo Pueblo, Kenneth M. Chapman, Laboratory of Anthropology Memoir I, Santa Fe, 1939.

A History of the Ancient Southwest, H. S. Gladwin, Bond Wheelright Co., Portland, Maine, 1957.

Pueblo Indian Pottery: Materials, Tools and Techniques, Marjorie F. Lambert, Museum of New Mexico Press, Santa Fe, 1966.

Southwest Indian Craft Arts, Clara Lee Tanner, University of Arizona Press, Tucson, 1968.

The Pottery of San Ildefonso Pueblo, Kenneth M. Chapman and Francis H. Harlow, School of American Research, Santa Fe, 1970.

Matte-Paint Pottery of the Tewa, Keres and Zuñi Pueblos, Francis H. Harlow, Museum of New Mexico Press, Santa Fe, 1973.

Historic Pottery of the Pueblo Indians, 1600–1880, Larry Frank and Francis H. Harlow, New York Graphic Society, Boston, 1974.

Seven Families in Pueblo Pottery, Maxwell Museum of Anthropology, Albuquerque, 1974.

Pottery Treasures, Jerry Jacka and Spencer Gill, Graphic Arts Center Publishing Co., Portland, Oregon, 1976.

Pueblo Pottery of the New Mexico Indians, Betty Toulouse, Museum of New Mexico Press, Santa Fe, 1977.

INDEX

Acoma, 2, 7, 12, 13, 14, 15, 16, 38, 52, 54, 66, 74–82, 85, 87, 88
Anaya, Josefita, 44
Aragon, W., 78
Arizona, 2
Ashiwi area, 85
Atencio, Luteria, 26
Avanyu, 36
Bandelier, Adolph, 34
Basketmakers, 11
Bearpaw design, 28, 29, 30
Casas Grandes, 8, 102, 104
Cata, Bettie, 24
Cata, Mary R., 26
Cata, Regina, 27
Cata, Rosita, 27
Chihuahua, 102
Classic Period, 14
Cochiti, 15, 17, 34, 35, 50–61, 64, 78, 88, 100, 103
Cody, Art, 33
Colorado, 11
Commercial Decline Period, 15
Commercial Revival Period, 15
Cordero, Helen, 50, 57
Da, Popovi, 35, 37, 41
Da, Tony, 41
Decline and Transition Period, 15
Derek, iv
Early Historic Period, 13
European influence, 13
Fawn, 94
Fields, Annie, 98
Forms and uses of pottery, 7
Glaze, 3, 12, 13, 75, 82, 104
Glossary, 103

Gonzales, Rose, 37, 38
Gutierrez, Lela, 28
Gutierrez, Luther, 28, 29
Gutierrez, Margaret, 28
Gutierrez, V., 43
Gutierrez, Van, 28
Hano, 15, 91
Historic Era, 13
Hopi, 7, 8, 10, 12, 14, 52, 85, 87, 90–95
Incised style, 27
Indian market, 16, 65, 71
Isleta, 51, 65, 82, 83
Jemez, 10, 13, 14, 62–65, 69
Keres area, Northeast, 15, 51
Laguna, 10, 14, 15, 16, 66, 81–83
Legoria, 32
Lewis, Lucy M., 74, 80
Lois, iv
Lonewolf, Joseph, 32
Lowden, Anita, 79
MacCallum, Spencer, 102
Manufacture of pottery, 2
Maricopa, 96, 97
Martinez, Adam, 41
Martinez, Crescencio, 35
Martinez, Julian, 16, 27, 35, 37, 41, 42
Martinez, Maria, 16, 27, 35, 36, 37, 39, 40, 41, 42
Martinez, Maximiliana, 35, 40
Martinez, Santana, 6, 37, 41
Medicine Flower, Grace, 32
Melcher, Crucita, 55
Melcher, Santana, 55
Mimbres, 8, 76, 104
Mojave, 98, 99
Montoya, Alfredo, 35, 39

Montoya, Clara, 36
Montoya, Dora, 66, 67
Montoya, Florentio, 35
Montoya, Martina, 35
Nambe, 15, 34, 43–45
Nampeyo, 15, 90, 91, 92, 93
Naranjo, Margaret, 31
Naranjo, Mrs., 30
National Recognition Period, 16
Navajo, 63, 81, 100, 101
New Mexico, 2, 34
Oraibi (Isleta), 82
Ortiz, Seferina, 78
Pacheco, Marie C., 57
Panana, Annie, 65
Panana, Luisa, 65
Papago, 99
Pecos, Nancy, 65
Petra, iv
Picuris, 20–23, 25, 44, 46
Pino, Dominguita, 36
Pino, Lorencita, 46, 48, 49
Pino, Vicentita, 71, 72
Poh've'ka, 37
Pojoaque, 34, 43, 44
Pottery manufacture, 2
Povika, 37
Prehistoric Era, 11
Pueblo Indians, 1, 11
Pueblo Revolt, 8, 51, 63, 81
Puname area, 14, 15, 63
Quezada, Juan, 102
"Rain god," 46, 47
Ranchitos, 65
Recent Period, 16
Rio Grande, 12, 13, 53, 69

INDEX

Roybal, Juan Cruz, 39
Roybal, Tonita, 36, 38, 39
San Felipe, 10, 14, 51, 52, 65, 69
San Ildefonso, 6, 15, 16, 27, 28, 34–42, 45, 53, 103
San Juan, 24–27
Santa Ana, 10, 51, 53, 63, 65–69
Santa Clara, 15, 25–34, 36, 38, 44, 103, 104
Santa Fe, 8, 16, 43, 52
Santa Fe Trail, 15, 34
Santo Domingo, 16, 34, 51–57, 88, 103
Sevenna, Seferina, 50, 57
Shutiva, Stella, 77
Sichomovi, 91
Stevenson, James, 21, 34, 56, 76, 87
Stone Age People, 2
Sunbird, iv
Swastika, 47, 101
Tafoya, Margaret, 28, 31
Tafoya, Severa, 28
Talachy, Joe, 44
Talachy, Thelma, 44
Taos, 21, 22, 44, 46
Tapia, Belen, 32
Tapia, Leonidas, 24
Tesuque, 9, 16, 34, 45–49, 53, 64, 88, 104
Tewa area, 14, 15, 21, 25, 103
Toya, Martha, 64
Trade routes, 15
Types of pottery, 6
Utilitarian Period, 14
Vigil, Priscilla, 45
Walpi, 91
Wedding jar, 29–31, 43, 47, 64, 94
Yepa, Juanita, 64
Yuma, 101
Zia, 2, 10, 15, 16, 17, 51, 53, 63, 64, 65, 66, 69–73, 75, 77, 82, 85, 86, 87, 88
Zuñi, 2, 6, 9, 10, 13, 14, 15, 16, 69, 71, 75, 78, 84–89, 104